Teenage
as a Second
Language

Teenage
as a Second
Language

A Parent's Guide to
Becoming Bilingual

Barbara R. Greenberg, PhD
and Jennifer A. Powell-Lunder, PsyD

Avon, Massachusetts

Published by
Adams Media, a division of F+W Media, Inc.
57 Littlefield Street, Avon, MA 02322. U.S.A.
www.adamsmedia.com

ISBN 10: 1-4405-0464-4
ISBN 13: 978-1-4405-0464-8
eISBN 10: 1-4405-0916-6
eISBN 13: 978-1-4405-0916-2

Printed in the United States of America.

10 9 8 7 6 5 4 3 2 1

Library of Congress Cataloging-in-Publication Data
Greenberg, Barbara R.
Teenage as a second language / Barbara R. Greenberg & Jennifer A. Powell-Lunder.
p. cm.
Includes index.
ISBN-13: 978-1-4405-0464-8
ISBN-13: 978-1-4405-0916-2 (ebk.)
ISBN-10: 1-4405-0464-4
ISBN-10: 1-4405-0916-6 (ebk.)
1. Teenagers—Language. 2. Body language. 3. Communication. I. Powell-Lunder, Jennifer
A. II. Title.
P120.Y68G74 2010
408.35—dc22
2010027247

This book is available at quantity discounts for bulk purchases.
For information, please call 1-800-289-0963.

Dedication

This book is dedicated to our families who have stood behind us throughout this process.

It is equally dedicated to the hundreds of teens who let us into their lives and taught us to understand what they were saying.

Acknowledgments

This book started as a discussion at the kitchen table between two good friends who happen to be psychologists. We began this journey with nothing but the knowledge that we needed to write this book. Starting with only a title, we watched as this project truly took on a life of its own. We thank the following people who offered direction, inspiration, and support. Without them we would still be sitting at the kitchen table.

To Jeanne Fredericks our amazing agent and guide.

To Paula Munier at Adams Media for her enthusiasm and commitment.

To Katie Corcoran Lytle at Adams Media because no question was too small or unimportant.

We are indebted to the following people: Lisa Green, John Silbersack, Laura Nolan, Janet Segal, Bill Lunder, Sydney Lunder, Barrett Lunder, Sherry Powell, Ronald Powell, Jonathan Powell, Bob Lunder, Angie Lunder, Linda Sussman, Tracy Schofield, Amanda Harvey, Ted Jonathan, Douglas Anderson, Derek Anderson, Pearl Green, Jayne Stein, Sharon Green, Mitch Greenberg, and Amy Foster.

Contents

Introduction

Fine. Whatever. I don't care. These can be the most frustrating words that parents ever hear. "What do they even mean?" you may be asking yourself. As parents you sometimes misunderstand what your teenagers are really trying to say and often find yourselves unable to respond effectively. Your children are at an age where you are encouraging them to express themselves, but you are unfortunately unable to understand their language. But there is hope. Throughout this book, we will teach you to translate what your teens actually say in English to what they really mean in *Teenage*. In an honest, clear, and concise manner, we combine our own experience working with parents and teenagers with the most current research on parent–teenage communication and explain how to really understand—and talk to—your teens.

The benefit isn't just a better relationship with your children. Research consistently concludes that both the quantity and quality of the communication between teenagers and parents affects teenage decision-making. It is evident that teens make healthier decisions, cope better with peer pressure, and have higher self-esteem when their parents positively and consistently talk to them about sensitive topics such as safe sex and drug use. In fact, adults who characterized their teenage years as marked by positive communication with their parents report a higher quality of life as adults in comparison to those who were unable to communicate well with their parents as teens.

This quick and easy reference will serve as your guide to understanding your teenagers. You'll learn how to become your teenagers' confidante, translate nonverbal communication such as changes in dress or behavior, and know when or if to worry and how to react. We'll also help you figure out how to interpret requests for more independence; understand, manage, and prevent the negative effects which can result from keeping secrets and telling lies; and initiate communication regarding sensitive topics. Within each chapter you will find easy-to-read tables and lists providing you with the information and tools you need to talk to your teens. Use them as reference guides to teach and reinforce your *Teen* communication skills. You will also find *Get Them Talking* segments, which serve as quick conversation starters, scattered throughout the text. In addition, we've included *Teen Speak* segments that provide you with commonly misunderstood words, phrases, and nonverbal language to help you proceed on your journey toward fluency.

It's important to keep in mind that, when learning any new language, the first few lessons are usually the most difficult. The more *Teenage* you learn the more competent you will feel. The bottom line is that when you are able to communicate effectively with your teenagers, both they—and you!—will feel better about yourselves, your relationships, and the future. So use this book as your guide and get ready for an immersion course in *Teenage*.

Good luck!

CHAPTER 1

Getting Started—Teenage 101: Understanding the Basics on the Road Toward Fluency

Take a moment to think back to your own adolescence. You may recall carefree days when your only responsibilities included completing your homework on time and perhaps working a part-time job to earn some fun money. Now spend some time talking to your teens. We can assure you that they will use many adjectives to describe their experiences but *carefree* will not be one of them! Clearly with all of our new technological advances—texting, Facebook, iPods, etc.—things have gotten a bit more complicated. The point? Each of our experiences is relative.

There is a strong chance (especially if you are reading this book) that your teenagers believe you do not have a clue about how difficult and complicated life is for them. You may actually feel the same way about their perceptions of your life! Believe it or not, some of their belief systems can be attributed to plain old biology. So, keeping this in mind, let's focus quickly on adolescent development before delving into how to understand their language.

What Happened to My Baby?

While there continues to be much debate regarding the age at which adolescence officially ends, most agree that the beginning of adolescence is marked by the start of puberty. Recently called the *tween years*—or the *mean years* by some parents—this period begins at around ten or eleven for girls and up to two years later for boys. During this time you may find yourself asking, "Who is this ornery child? I want my baby back!" Hopefully, the realization that you are not alone in your questioning or wishful thinking will give you some solace. That said, take a deep breath. Once puberty has started there is no looking back! With changes in the body come stressors such as changes in mood, appearance, and attitude. However, some of you may be surprised and quite relieved to learn that the generally accepted idea that adolescent angst (e.g., intense moodiness) continues in full force throughout adolescence has actually proven to be mostly myth. While changing hormones may produce emotional imbalance in tweens, by the time they reach their mid-teen years most kids have learned to regulate their moods. You may be shaking your head. After all, you know moodiness when you see it. Read on however, and you may realize that many of your teens' reactions may be attributed less to hormonal changes and more to their developmentally appropriate belief systems that can result in emotional responses including annoyance, frustration, embarrassment, and even sadness.

An additional stressor, especially for girls, is maturing early—which can lead to compromised self-esteem and poor body image. Thankfully, parents who offer love and support through comfort and open communication can counteract this stress. In short, talking to your teens about these early changes can really make a difference. Listening in a caring and empathic manner can help ensure that your teens' self-esteem and perceptions of self remain positive and intact.

GET THEM TALKING

"That would bother me if it happened to me."

By being empathic and supportive you are more likely to get your teens to talk to you.

Adolescence is also a time when teens search for an identity and try on different roles. "A ha," you think, "That is why he is walking out the door looking like a metal-band roadie one minute, and a California surfer dude the next." A momentary reflection on your own teen years may bring a quick chuckle as you recall the different roles you played.

On occasion a mother will come to us distressed and concerned because her teen has suddenly re-designed her life plan. "For as long as I can remember," the parent will tell us "she has wanted to be an attorney like her father and I. Now suddenly she has decided she is going to go to college out west so that she can become a ski instructor once she graduates!" Our advice? Hold back the urge to criticize. Listen to her hopes and dreams, as disappointing or unrealistic as they may sound. By keeping an open mind and listening to her ideas in an uncritical manner you send the message that you respect her, and you teach her that anything is possible. A major highlight of the teen years is working through the pull to become an independent adult and the push to remain a dependent child. (See Chapter 4 for more.) Your teens will have plenty of time to work out whether the goals they have set for themselves are attainable or realistic. Remember, these are their lives, not yours.

While He Is the Center of My Universe, Why Does He Believe the Universe Revolves Around Him?

Okay, you guessed it, your teen's self-absorption and egocentrism are developmentally appropriate and on target. Hard to believe, we know, but it's the truth just the same. This tendency toward self-focus occurs because, as noted above, during adolescence, teens are actively searching to find their identities. Because they believe that the world revolves around them, they also believe the world is always watching them. This, in part, explains why your daughter may become hysterical when she notices a new pimple on her face the night of the big dance. While you may have to squint to even see the blemish in question, we forewarn you that your reassurance is likely to go nowhere; she will be convinced that while you may be blind, the rest of the world has 20/20 vision! This self-focus may also explain why your son turns a bright red shade of embarrassed when your husband tells corny jokes to your son's friends.

Sound familiar? Well, there are lots of other ways that your teen's egocentrism affects how he looks at the world—or even you!

It's Personal So You Couldn't Possibly Understand

Have you begun to wonder why you receive blank stares every time you try to relate to your teens by offering a story from your experiences? If you are really lucky your teens may actually verbalize what they are thinking, "You have no idea how I feel!" Rest assured that it is not that things have really changed so much since you were a teenager. This behavior is actually developmental as well. Teens truly believe that the things they think and feel belong only to them. They believe that no one, especially their parents, could ever even begin to know what it is like to walk in their shoes. In time, as they move into adulthood they will start to appreciate your expressions of empathy and understanding, but now is not the time. Our suggestion: Don't take it personally!

Thought and Reason

As your teens continue to grow and develop you will no doubt notice all of the wonderful things that go along with maturity. As their brains develop so do their abilities to think and reason. It is exciting to listen to your teens express their opinions and offer their world views. They now possess the ability to actively participate in political conversations and can reason intelligently about causes for which they are passionate. It is for this reason that they may protest sitting at the kid's table this Thanksgiving, or offer an opinion at the dinner table on subjects about which they seemed disinterested or clueless only months before. Your teens are able at this point to express their opinions and share their knowledge. Now is the time to seek out your teens and ask them to explain and demonstrate how to use all those amazing features on your new cell phone, program your new Blu-ray player, or enhance your Facebook pages or YouTube videos. Believe it or not, these capacities are all related to their developing brains; at this stage in development their abilities to take in new information and learn from experiences are at their peak.

The fact that your teens are more likely than ever before to challenge your arguments for or against things is also tied to this developmental stage. The old "because I said so," may not work as well as it used to. As with any new ability, adolescents are eager to use their newfound abstract thinking and deductive reasoning skills. Many parents report, however, that their teens often use these skills to argue against the rationale for decisions made by their parents. This is where creating a clear set of collaborative rules and consequences can come in handy. (More on that in *Setting the Rules* later in this chapter.)

FINE:

1. I will reluctantly consent, but not with pleasure.
PARENT: "Please do your homework."
TEENAGER: "Fine!"
SUGGESTED PARENTAL RESPONSE: None needed. You have made your wishes known.

2. An intentionally vague description used when a teenager clearly has no interest in providing further detail.
PARENT: "How was school today?"
TEENAGER: "Fine!"
SUGGESTED PARENTAL RESPONSE: Let the teen know that you are available later to talk. For example: "Now is probably not a good time to talk. Just let me know if you want to talk later."

Masters of Their Domains

Adolescence is also a time when self-esteem can be vulnerable. You may notice that the tween who wanted to participate in everything from art and music classes to baseball has slowly (or in some cases quickly) begun to narrow his interests. He may no longer want to practice piano or play club basketball. Don't feel guilty if you feel some secret relief from this choice because you know he wasn't that good at those activities to begin with. It is in fact because of his struggle with those activities that he has probably stopped.

Because these years are so tied to self-concern and self-focus, teens want to feel confident and competent about the things they do—and don't we all? They, therefore, often narrow their focuses to activities that make them feel masterful. These activities, of course, tend to be ones at which they are good. The structure of their lives also helps encourage this process. For example, if your daughter is a good athlete but wants to play two sports that have overlapping seasons, she will most likely have to drop one. She will probably choose to continue the sport at which she feels most competent. Other elements will factor into her decision however. Because what others think of her is so important to her at this point in her life, she will also weigh both your opinion and the opinions of her peers when making the choice. She may pick according to her skill level and her social comfort. The number of friends she has on each team may also influence her decision.

The Many Faces of Your Teens

As your teens begin to grow and hone their skills in different areas, they develop impressions about themselves in these areas. Just as the black-and-white thinking of childhood becomes more abstract and complex, so do your teens' perceptions of self. This all translates into teens who may seem competent and confident in one area but not another. Your daughter for example, may seem secure and outgoing when she is with you or her friends, however she may appear shy and anxious in math class. This also explains why you are sometimes surprised when you attend teacher conferences, or get feedback from other parents about your teens. The teen you see is probably not the teen everyone sees. The picture portrayed is dependent on the situations and how equipped your teens feel in handling the specific environments.

GET THEM TALKING

"What songs did the band play at the concert?"
This is an indirect request for information about how the night went. You are more likely to get a conversation started if you try this style.

A Little Encouragement Goes a Long Way

Many parents report that they feel that their adolescents aren't interested in their opinions or suggestions; again, this is in part due to teens' natural inclinations to believe that no one—especially their parents—can possibly understand or relate to how they think and feel. However, despite your teens' dismissals of your recommendations, it is important to understand that how you perceive them matters now more than ever. Although your teens may lead you to believe that your compliments and words of encouragement bounce right off of them, do not be fooled. This type of support is more powerful than you can imagine. Ignore the fact that your teens may have difficulties accepting your positive feedback. For example, when you tell your daughter that she looks beautiful and she responds, "You're supposed to say that, you're my mother," pat yourself on the back because what she is telling you is that you are doing your job. Imagine how she would feel if you didn't say these things to her.

WHATEVER:

1. An expression that implies that a teen may give in but is not really interested in what is being said.
PARENT: "We are going to visit your Great Aunt today."
TEENAGER: "Whatever."
SUGGESTED PARENTAL RESPONSE: Leave this alone. Do not let your own concern that your teen may be less than thrilled create an unnecessary controversy.

2. An attempt to be dismissive in as few words as possible.
PARENT: "Why don't you call Emma, she seems so nice?"
TEENAGER: "Whatever!"
SUGGESTED PARENTAL RESPONSE: Let it go, no topic is as important as the quality of your relationship with your teen.

See Yourself the Way You Want Them to See Themselves

Another essential element in supporting your teens' self-esteem, is viewing yourself in a positive light. If you have a tendency to make negative comments about yourself or highlight your own weaknesses at the cost of emphasizing your strengths, the message you send your teens may far outweigh the benefits of any verbal reinforcement you offer. Remember, your teens look to you to model appropriate behaviors. By consistently acknowledging your own competencies you suggest that you possess a positive self-image and teach your teens that this self-view is the norm. Therefore, parents who see themselves as confident and competent deliver more valuable verbal messages to their children than parents with low self-esteem. Those positive verbal messages reinforce the way they portray themselves. Bottom line, if you feel good about yourself, you help your teens feel good about themselves. Although your words may feel like they are falling on deaf ears, they are really meaningful and important.

I Understand That He Feels Like He Could Fly but Why Does He Want to Jump Out of a Plane Without a Parachute to Prove This?

At this point you may be feeling a little confused. "Why," you may be wondering, "does my teen sometimes engage in highly risky behaviors if he now has the reasoning ability to understand the potential consequences?" By asking this question you are in good company; developmental theorists have often pondered this question. While no definitive answer can be offered there are several theories that make a lot of sense. One thought is that although your teens certainly have the ability to identify and understand potential consequences their egocentric thinking makes them believe that these consequences apply only to others. Your daughter for example, may have no problem advising her brother not to stay up all night before a big test, and yet, when you happen to walk by her room at midnight the night before her exam, you hear her chatting or tapping away on her cell phone.

Another explanation for lapses in judgment may simply be due to selective reasoning. It has been proposed that teens pick and choose the information they will attend to depending on the situations in which they find themselves. "I can stay on the phone. I already know this stuff. I don't need to study."

It is also thought that adolescents are sometimes willing to take risky chances because they lack the impulse control possessed by adults. Finally, teens may believe that the immediate rewards of a potentially risky behavior far outweigh the potential negative consequences, "I would much rather hear about Maddy's breakup with Dale than study. Besides, even if I don't do well on this exam, it is so early in the quarter, I can make it up on another exam, or do extra credit." In short, teens are often willing to take risks because they feel like they have the world at their feet. Remember that feeling? One has to admit, it was truly amazing.

The ESP Factor

You now know what you need to about adolescent development, but you still need to learn about the fundamental ideas underlying how to speak *Teenage*. Start by asking yourself these questions: Are you often one step ahead of your teens? Do you frequently feel like you know exactly what they are going to do even before they do? For example:

MOTHER: "Don't even think about it."
TEENAGER: "But Mom!"
MOTHER: "Don't 'but' me. I said no."

If the interaction above sounds even remotely familiar then you have contributed to what we call the *ESP Factor*—the false belief that parents always know what their children are thinking, feeling, or doing. In reality, of course, parents do not always know this information and this false assumption can lead to miscommunication. The *ESP Factor* is, in fact, a two-way street. It can result in both teens and parents thinking that the other has this supernatural ability to read their minds. Either way, this false sense of clairvoyance between parent and child is a driving force behind the miscommunication that results in a mistranslation of *Teenage*.

Where Does It Start?

Before we go any further, let's take a step back in an effort to understand where the phenomenon begins. As a new parent, you likely struggled to understand your infant's wants and needs. So much of those early days was spent trying to decipher what every sound from crying to cooing meant. You eagerly watched your child's facial expressions and body language, anxious to fulfill every need. This anxiety is evident when you to talk to new parents. You may chuckle as one parent tells you she is worried because her son sleeps too much, while another parent complains that his daughter does not sleep enough. Those early days are spent learning the language of your baby, "Is that loud shriek a cry for hunger or does it mean a diaper is wet?" Whether it took days or even months, with the acquisition of this new language came a sense of confidence—perhaps too much confidence.

Your understanding of your children's language continued throughout their childhood. You may have felt so fluent that you often knew what your children wanted or needed before they uttered a single word. As a result, you could sometimes head off difficult situations or prevent them from entering harm's way. As your confidence in your ability to understand your children grew so did their confidence in your ability to know what they wanted or needed. This confidence, however, can result in a false sense of awareness and understanding. It leaves your children truly believing that you know all.

GET THEM TALKING

"You have to try this chocolate cake."
You are making yourself available and not demanding information. In these situations your teens may just start chatting.

While adolescent egocentrism may result in your teens believing that you could not possibly understand what they think and feel, the *ESP Factor* leaves them feeling confused and frustrated when you don't, which can lead to misunderstandings and miscommunication. At other times, the factor leads to situations during which your teens are convinced that you know what they are doing. Here, your silence is interpreted as tacit agreement. As we are sure you can imagine, this misperception can lead to concerning and occasionally dangerous situations and can leave teens feeling like their parents do not know them at all.

If You Say It Be Sure You Mean It

The flip side of the *ESP Factor* results in parents believing that their teens have the ability to accurately discern what they (the parents) mean at all times. An example that comes to our minds is parents' misperception that their teens know when they are being sarcastic. We can't begin to recall how many times the teens we have worked with have related scenarios similar to the one that we present below.

In this scenario, a parent becomes frustrated with his son because he is not doing well in math. When he comes upon his son he is chatting with his friends on the computer or playing a game.

FATHER: "Don't you think you should be working on your math homework?"
SON: "I was, I am just taking a break."
FATHER: "A break, oh that's good, take a break! Take all the time you need!"

The son then goes back to what he was doing. His father checks in a few minutes later and sees him still not doing his homework.

FATHER: "What are you doing? With study habits like that, no wonder your grades are poor! Why aren't you studying? Didn't we already have this conversation? Didn't I tell you to put that away and hit the book?"
SON: "But, Dad, you said I could take a break."

FATHER: "Didn't you hear a word I said?" (yelling) "That's it. I am taking away your computer. If you want to fail, go ahead, but your mother and I are not going to have any part of it!"

Both father and son are left feeling frustrated and upset.

Diagnosing the Problem

Children learn to respect the authority of their parents. They rely on you to clearly define what is expected of them. As your children grow older you begin to recognize the shift in their thinking and respond to their increasing maturity. For example, you may assume that your teens know when you are being straightforward and when you are being sarcastic. However, you may sometimes fail to realize that your teens tend to take you literally because they have been taught to do so and, as you see in the dialogue above, these misunderstandings can lead to frustration and even anger.

When you use sarcasm you send a confusing message. If your teens are programmed to do what you say, they cannot be expected to suddenly know when you do not mean what you say. Remember, so much of your teens' self-esteem is related to their earlier experiences—which you played a pivotal role in—and it is easier for them to go back to default and just follow directions, especially in an emotionally charged situation. While your teens may be smart enough to know when you are being sarcastic, intellect is not the skill on which they rely when interactions become heated. In the midst of an argument it is best to avoid sending mixed messages. One way to avoid the confusion is that you should *say what you mean and mean what you say* at all times. If you're having difficulty refraining from sarcasm during an argument, consider using the following examples as inspiration:

TRY THIS	RATHER THAN THIS
"You have had your break. Now please go back to studying. Feel free to ask me if you want me to help you study or understand something."	"You know what? Forget it. You don't care. You're right. Take a break. Take all the breaks in the world."
"Right now I am very angry. Please go to your room, we will talk about this later."	"That's it. Pack your bags. If you don't like it, you can leave."
"You cannot go out tonight until you clean up your room."	"Sure you can go out. You want to live in a pigsty, go ahead. Maybe while you're gone your room will clean itself!"

So then the question clearly becomes, how do you ensure that you and your teen are truly speaking the same language without relying solely on the intuition associated with the *ESP Factor*? This is where rules and guidelines become not only recommended but necessary. Rules serve to head off situations when the *ESP Factor* fails.

Setting Rules

Imagine after a series of interviews you finally land your dream job. Next, imagine that when you inquire about work hours and benefits such as vacation time and health insurance, you are met with vague responses such as "We'll see how it goes," or "Whatever." Now imagine that when you ask for a clear definition of your job title and description of duties you are met with, "You'll figure it out," or "I'm not sure." "You're not sure," you think to yourself, "then who is?" It is doubtful that you would allow yourself to leave the situation—or even accept the job—without getting answers to these important questions.

Now imagine that you are a teenager. You tell your parents that you are going out for the evening and ask them what time they'd like you to return. They respond "Whenever." They do not ask you where you are going or with whom. If you are a teen, at first you may think, "Cool." However, if you stop and think you may ask yourself "Don't they care where I am going? Aren't they concerned about what I may be doing and what time I am coming back?"

NOT:

1. A word that unambiguously implies that the teen is not interested.

PARENT: "I signed you up for art lessons."

TEENAGER: "Not!"

SUGGESTED PARENTAL RESPONSE: Take a breath and calmly ask your teen why this is not a good idea. Caution: Avoid a struggle by refraining from an angry response.

2. A clear expression of refusal.

PARENT: "You are going to that camp again this summer."

TEENAGER: "Not."

SUGGESTED PARENTAL RESPONSE: Use this as an opportunity to inquire further. In the above example a parent might respond: "Oh, I'm sorry, I thought you liked camp. Fill me in."

We all need rules and structure. Most kids, especially adolescents, thrive in structured and predictable situations. Rules offer explanations about which behaviors are appropriate and what is expected of us. They also define boundaries, without which the world would feel chaotic and unsafe. In addition, rules take the emotion out of the equation and tell us what is expected. As our children get older the rules should certainly grow with them, but they should not, however, be eliminated.

When Parents Aren't Anxious, Life Is Beautiful!

Sometimes the hardest thing about introducing a formalized set of rules is selling the concept to your teenager. Teens fight hard for their independence and the idea of predetermined rules may sound threatening—especially if this is a new proposal. Just because their initial reactions may not be welcoming, do not be discouraged. As parents you have to remember that teens are *supposed* to fight against the idea of rules and, in reality, teens from homes with structure and rules fare far better than teens from unstructured, permissive homes.

Our mantra to teens is this: "When your parents aren't anxious, life is beautiful." We explain that parents worry about their kids—no matter their ages—and when parents worry they tend to respond in reactive and sometimes negative ways. Rules help to alleviate stress for both parents and teens because they ensure that everyone knows what is expected. In reality, the issue is not whether or not to put rules into place, but how they are put into place that makes all the difference!

Writing the Rules—No Need to Bring Your Attorney

The task of writing rules should be an interactive one. When working with families we recommend that teens and parents each come to the table with a written set of rules and consequences. Before creating this list you and your teens should discuss some of the hot topics in the home that require rules. In our experience this may include rules regarding curfew, room cleaning, computer use, car use, etc. Do not create rules for the sake of creating rules. If your teen routinely and satisfactorily cleans her room, for example, then there is no need to make a rule about this. Rules should be created regarding safety issues such as where your teens go and how they get ther, etc.

The goal here is to create a structured and predictable home environment and it is important to acknowledge that this is an interactive process. When teens are fully involved in the process of creating the rules they feel empowered; they are more likely to comply with the rules because to some degree they will feel like they own them. This heads off such protests as: "I don't have to follow those rules. I didn't agree to them, those are *your* rules."

Your teens should also be encouraged to discuss and develop guidelines for you if necessary. For example, we commonly get complaints from teens about their parents snooping around their rooms, barging into their rooms without warning or provocation, or listening in on phone conversations. One teen even took this issue beyond the idea of privacy and complained that her parents routinely fed their dog at the table! We are not suggesting that you allow your teens to rule the home. We simply want you and your teens to use this opportunity to address as many issues as possible, especially those that result in conflict and discord.

When developing the rules you and your partner should have one list of rules and consequences and present as a unified front. It is important that you discuss this list together and fully agree on what you are presenting before coming to the table. This will keep you from getting sidetracked in the process. It also prevents splitting—when one parent seems like the good cop and the other the bad cop.

The more precisely the rule is written, the better. If there is a rule about cleaning the room, for example, it should clearly state the day of the week and time by which the room should be cleaned. In addition, the definition of *clean* should be clearly outlined. *Clean* to your teens may mean shoving everything under the bed or in the closet, whereas to you it may mean things are put in specific places. For every rule there should be a clearly defined consequence. If the rule states that the room must be cleaned by 5:00 P.M. on Friday, it must be understood that at 5:01 P.M. the agreed upon consequence automatically occurs. In addition, this also means that if at 4:59 P.M. the room is still not cleaned, you refrain from saying or doing anything until 5:01 P.M. We realize it may be difficult for some of you to follow this rule, which is exactly why we strongly suggest laying out these guidelines ahead of time.

The conflicts between you and your teens may arise because your teens feel that you are nagging them to do something. It may come as a surprise that when your teens feel you are nagging them, it only serves to make them *not* want to do whatever it is that is being requested. Teens report that when parents consistently remind them to do something, it sends a message that their parents don't trust them or don't think that they are capable of completing the tasks on their own. Their thinking becomes "Fine, if you won't leave me alone, then, I won't do it!" However, again, the guidelines we are suggesting take the emotion out of the equation. When you and your teens agree on a rule and a consequence all parties are held accountable. We realize that for some of you the thought of refraining from offering a reminder or two to your teens about specific chores may produce overwhelming anxiety. That is why we suggest that friendly reminders be incorporated into specific rules. You and your teens can agree, for example, that you can offer a set number of reminders prior to the pre-established chore deadline. Each rule can have the same consequence if all agree that it is an effective deterrent to breaking the rule.

Coming to the Table

Teens should present their list of rules and consequences first. We recommend allowing them to present the whole list and then go through each rule one by one. You may be surprised to discover that the rules listed by your teens may be very similar to corresponding rules on your lists and that the consequences on your teens' lists may be far more severe than the consequences you've listed. No matter whose consequence you choose to go with, it's important that they are realistic. If the rule dictates that your teens must be in by a certain hour for curfew and the consequence is too severe (such as grounding for two months—a lifetime to your teens—after one offense), the consequence can become worthless. Consequences carry more impact if they are immediate and enforceable. Too often we work with teens who end up consistently breaking the same rule because they feel the consequence put them in a hopeless situation. "I'll never be able to go out so I might as well just do it anyway." In addition, a rule is only as good as the commitment to keep it enforced. A common breakdown occurs when parents inconsistently implement consequences. This sends the message that you are not invested in the process. It should be understood that if a rule is broken the consequence automatically goes into effect, no questions asked, no emotion involved.

GET THEM **TALKING**

"It's so discouraging to make that kind of mistake. Isn't it?"

If you are tolerant of mistakes you can expect an honest conversation.

The rules and consequences you create should be written and posted in a place where everyone has access to them. The process of actually writing down the rules makes them real. A system should also be established to discuss and revisit rules that are not working. Think of this as an ongoing interactive process. If a rule or consequence is not helpful or enforceable, do not get stuck. Rules were meant to be rewritten. They should serve as helpful guidelines and become useless if they are not realistic.

It is important to discuss with your teens that there will be situations for which no rule currently exists. In these cases your teens need to defer to your judgment, especially if the issue involves potential safety risks. This can be difficult for your teens to understand because again, your perception of high-risk situations may not be consistent with their perceptions. However, it must be clarified that your concerns for your teens' safety trump any existing rules.

Rules for Difficult Circumstances

We truly believe that this interactive rule-making process encourages open communication and helps teens feel empowered in their own homes. However, while we believe in developing rules *together*, there are several rules we recommend for teens struggling with difficult situations such as drug or alcohol abuse. When establishing these rules with your teens it is important to explain that they are not being implemented as a punishment but rather as opportunities to ensure safety and repair the trust that has been broken.

The Money Rule

This rule states that all money acquired by your teen must be accounted for and given to parents. When money is needed parents will decide the appropriate amount given the nature of the request. Upon return home, all money spent must be accounted for—receipts should be expected when possible. Why do we recommend this rule? Let's be honest, drugs and alcohol cost money. We realize you may never have envisioned yourself in the role of an accountant, especially with your teens. We understand that this is a labor-intensive task and that you may be thinking it would be easier to simply refrain from giving any money to your teens and instead to make all purchases for them. In fact, we do suggest that *when* your teens protest this rule (and the others that follow) you offer this suggestion. Most teens—when given the choice—will opt for some control rather than none.

The Random Stop-By Rule

This rule states that your teens should be prepared that you will be randomly stopping by to make sure they are where they say they are. Don't be surprised if your teens react with terror after hearing this one. It is important to further explain that your goal is not to embarrass your teens around their friends, just to restore the trust that has been lost. Explain further that whenever possible you will be subtle when checking up; in fact, we recommend that you caution that she might not even know you were there. "How is this done," you ask? For example, if your teen states that she is going to the 8:00 P.M. movie with her friends, surreptitiously confirm her presence at the theater at the indicated time and quietly leave. Later when they arrive home be direct and let her know you were there. This sends the message that although you are following through checking up, you really are trying to refrain from embarrassing or shaming her in front of her friends. When your teens have been where they were supposed to be, praise them and let them know that this reinforces your trust in them.

The Random Room Check Rule

It is not uncommon for parents to want to search their teens' rooms. Our role is *not* to tell you whether we recommend room searches. Instead, we are here to explain to you how to do this if you choose this course of action. Teenagers thrive on privacy; our experience is that most teens consider their rooms their inner sanctums. This is why most teens take such offense when their parents search their rooms. We know of many parents who have tried to avoid confrontation with their teens by not telling them they have been searching. Well, we would be willing to bet that your teen already has an inkling that you have been in there snooping and one of the major messages you send to your teens with this behavior is that it is okay to do things in secret (more on this is Chapter 5). We suggest that if you have made the decision to randomly search your teens' room that you follow these guidelines.

Inform your teens of this decision. It is important that you also indicate that after the discussion you will be doing a search immediately. Tell your teens that you understand that this feels like an invasion of privacy but you feel compelled to take this action in order to keep them safe. In addition, inform them that, while the searches will be random, you will only do a search when they are present. They can accompany you to their rooms but they cannot intervene. Let them know if they do intervene you will not allow them to be present during future searches. This protocol offers a mild sense of control to your teens in a situation in which they may feel humiliated and powerless. It is important to be respectful and remain focused. If you find items in their rooms that you did not expect to find (for example *Playboy*) do not address them in the moment. You can deal with these issues later. The goal is to remain focused on the task or goal.

Rules in Different Households

If your teens are living in two different households due to divorce or separation it is especially important that the rules are consistent between homes. This can reduce—and, in many cases, head off—conflict. For example, if rules are consistent you can avoid your teens' objections to rules such as "But in Dad's house I am allowed to." The process of parenting from separate homes can be difficult enough and consistent rules send the message that although you and your ex may have your differences, your are invested enough in your children to work together to ensure a structured and predictable home environment. This also avoids putting your teens in the middle of your conflicts with each other, a situation that can be quite damaging to kids of all ages. Remember this is about creating a safe, reliable home situation for your teens, not an opportunity to demonstrate who is the nicer or cooler parent.

Family Consequences: Sometimes Everyone Needs Some Redirection

While we are not suggesting that your teens provide *you* with consequences, on occasion we recommend a family consequence as a way to reshape the behavior of several or all the members of a family. Sometimes, for example, teens will tell us that they live in homes where yelling is common. This can be quite unsettling, as we are sure you can imagine. In addition, if you are modeling this behavior, you can expect your teens to follow suit. This creates an uncomfortable and loud home environment for everyone. In order to reduce yelling, the use of obscene language, or any other bad behavior that your family engages in we have suggested an intervention we call *The Money Jar*. Follow the steps below to put this technique into practice.

INTERVENTION: THE MONEY JAR

1. Place a large jar in a common area in the home (e.g., the kitchen).
2. Create a log sheet to record the name of the offender and the time and date of the offense.
3. Assign a monetary amount to the offense (e.g., a quarter for every offense).
4. Determine how long you will use the money pot. (We recommend one to three months.)
5. At the end of the predetermined time period check the log and count the money.
6. The family member with the least number of offenses gets the money in the jar.

If this is an issue you are seeking to address in your household, you may be amazed at the effectiveness of this technique. The key is that all family members have to acknowledge this as a problem and commit to the intervention. If the idea of putting money in a jar is not something that would work for your family, we recommend that you try a variation. Instead of putting money in the jar you can put slips of paper with the offending person's name. The slips of paper serve as vouchers or IOUs. Whoever has the most slips would then be required to do additional chores or tasks. If your teens have the least slips then they would be excused from certain chores.

Keep in mind though that nothing can totally prepare you for every situation that may arise. With a little ingenuity and forethought, however, you and your teens can work together to develop guidelines and rules in response to even the most unexpected of situations.

Would You Call 911 After a Crisis Is Over?

If you ask almost any five year old what three numbers they should call if there is a fire or an accident, they will frequently answer "911." That is because 911 is universal. Now imagine for a moment that 911 did not exist. Scary, right? We think it is fair to say that the concept behind 911 is brilliant. Calling those three numbers in the midst of a crisis allows one to feel empowered and reassured in a multitude of dangerous, chaotic, and life threatening situations. It also offers structure and predictability in situations in which both may be nonexistent. It seems logical, then, that a 911 or crisis plan should be created with your teens before a potential crisis occurs.

The older your teens become, the more independence they will probably seek (we discuss this in more detail in Chapter 4). By creating a general safety plan both you and your teens can feel more comfortable and confident as they venture out into the world on their own. Technology makes setting up a plan a no-brainer; often a one-word text message or phone call is the best choice. We suggest that you and your teens create a specific signal which means "Come get me, I need help." You and your teens must discuss ahead of time when the signal should be used as well as devise a backup plan in situations in which it may be ineffective (e.g., if either you or your teens may be in a bad cell zone or otherwise unreachable). It is also important to pre-establish the rules regarding use of the signal. We highly recommend that you agree ahead of time to respond to the crisis immediately, and ask questions regarding the situation at another time. For example, if your teen was drinking and doesn't feel he can drive, be grateful that he called or texted for a ride. We can assure you that if you spend the ride home yelling or lecturing him about underage drinking, it is highly unlikely that he will call you if it happens again. Sometimes the 911 signal may be initiated by your teens because they need you to help them help a friend. Again, be thankful that your teen felt comfortable enough to call you. Save the questions and lectures for later. Simply help them manage the situation at hand. We are not suggesting that you never address the situations. We are suggesting that it be agreed upon in advance that if the signal is given, you will respond to the crisis without judgment.

A Detailed Plan

A 911 plan does not always have to be just a one-word signal. You and your teens can also create more detailed 911 plans for specific situations that may present concerns ahead of time. If your teen is driving to a place she has never driven to before and is anxious about the directions prearranging a plan in case she gets lost can reduce the anxiety before it even begins. You may be thinking she could just use the GPS but your reassurance is probably more calming than a machine shouting out directions.

The process of devising a detailed 911 plan provides you and your teens an opportunity to discuss potential anxieties or concerns you both may be experiencing regarding an upcoming situation. Sometimes a 911 plan is simply a promise between you and your teens that you will be available to cheer on and or support them in a difficult situation. Some common situations may include: going to a job or college interview, taking a standardized test such as the ACT or the SAT, going out on a first date, or going to a big party. Sometimes the knowledge of the plans' existence can reduce so much anxiety and concern that it heads off a potential crisis.

NOSTRIL FLARING:

1. An attempt to convey anger and frustration.

PARENT: "Tell me everything about your day."

TEENAGER: Flares nostrils (may be accompanied by a glare).

SUGGESTED PARENTAL RESPONSE: Back off. Now is not the right time to gather information.

2. A response to a cold or an itchy nose.

PARENT: "Tell me everything about your day."

TEENAGER: Flares nostrils and then responds "It was good. I got my math test back . . . ."

SUGGESTED PARENTAL RESPONSE: Continue with listening and responding as usual. Your teenager's immediate response suggests that she is not in distress over your question.

When Words Don't Say It All

Throughout this book we will offer you strategies to manage even the simplest of interactions effectively, but before we proceed we'd like to offer a communication tool that can be implemented to satisfy your requests for information and your teens' reluctance to provide lengthy answers. However, before we go any further, let's consider the two scenarios presented below.

Scenario 1

PARENT 1: "Hi, honey, how was your day at school?"
TEENAGER: "Okay."
Several hours later the other parent arrives home from work.
PARENT 2: "How was Ava's day at school?"
PARENT 1: "Great!"

Scenario 2

PARENT 1: "Hi, honey, how was your day at school?"
TEENAGER: "Okay."
Several hours later the other parent arrives home from work.
PARENT 2: "How was Ava's day at school?"
PARENT 1: "Terrible!"

Confusing right? We agree. The answer to the question "How was your day at school" relies on the parent's interpretation of the response "Okay." In upcoming chapters we will offer you strategies to evoke more extensive and detailed information from your teens. But there are some times, however, when all you want to ensure is that things are going well. As you can see perception is everything so let's talk about a communication tool we call the *Feeling and Action Scale.*

I GET IT:

1. A phrase that simply implies that they understand.

PARENT: "The competition for college is going to be difficult so you should get your applications in early."

TEENAGER: "I get it."

SUGGESTED PARENTAL RESPONSE: None. This seems like a moment of attunement.

2. A phrase that describes an "aha" moment.

PARENT: "So, if you do it like this it makes it easier."

TEENAGER: "I get it!"

SUGGESTED PARENTAL RESPONSE: Just smile, your enthusiasm says it all.

3. An expression of frustration because the teen feels doubted.

PARENT: "Remember to check the deadlines."

TEENAGER: "I get it!"

SUGGESTED PARENTAL RESPONSE: Try to neutralize your child's response with a calm answer. For the example above: "Good. Now you will be ahead of the game."

Implementing the Feeling and Action Scale

The *Feeling and Action Scale* is a two-part communication tool. The first part, the *Feeling Scale*, consists of a range of numbers from 1–5. For each number assigned, your teens also assign a one-word qualifier to describe how they are feeling in the moment or to describe their overall feelings about a situation or event. A 1 on the scale signifies that all is well, while a 5 indicates that your teen is experiencing a crisis. We'll take another look at the scenario above to see how this scale can help you out.

PARENT 1: "Hi, honey, how was your day at school?"
TEENAGER: "A one."
PARENT 1: "I'm happy to hear that."

While we suggest the *Feeling Scale* as a tool for you and your teens, we recommend that all family members use the scale as a way to quickly check in with each other. It is especially helpful when you use the scale to describe your own feelings to your teens after a difficult day. Because your teens are prone to egocentric thinking, when they perceive that you are not in a good mood, they often assume that they have done something to make you feel this way. If you can quickly clarify your emotional state to your teens, it can prevent them from feeling stress and concern. The scenario below demonstrates how the scale can be helpful in this manner.

TEENAGER: "Hi, Mom. When is dinner going to be ready?"
PARENT: "Hi, Honey. I'm a four right now because of a situation at work, so I just need a minute to relax."
TEENAGER: "No problem."

The second part of the scale focuses on actions. The *Action Scale* is a set of instructions that can help you help your teens when they are dealing with difficult feelings. For each feeling qualifier there should be an action, even if the action is "no action." It is important to recognize that there should be several action alternatives for each feeling. The ability to implement a specific action will, of course, be dependent on the situation. If, for example, you are driving somewhere with your teen and she announces that she is a "four" and "four" usually means "I need to be alone," be prepared to improvise. If your daughter has an iPod in the car suggest that she "take alone time" by tuning everything else out while she tunes in her music. Below we offer an example of how a completed scale could look.

THE FEELING AND ACTION SCALE:

1. I'm great = No action needed.
2. I'm fine = No action needed.
3. I'm so so = I need some alone time in my room.
4. I'm upset = I need some alone time and then I want to talk with you about what is going on.
5. I'm in crisis = I need your help.

Congratulations! You have now learned the underlying principles necessary to start talking *Teenage*—and more is yet to come!

The following is a recap of some of the most important basic concepts to remember as you continue to build on your knowledge of *Teenage.*

1. **Adolescent Angst May be Part Myth:** The beginning of puberty can bring with it what is often characterized as adolescent moodiness. But the strong emotional reactions you may observe your teen experiencing toward certain situations may be attributed to a set of developmentally appropriate beliefs.

2. **"Me, Me, Me," Is Developmentally Appropriate:** Adolescent egocentrism results in a self-focused belief system. Teens assume that the world is watching their every move. They are convinced that no one has ever thought or felt the way they do and may feel as though they are invincible.

3. **Leave Clairvoyance to the Fortune Teller:** The *ESP Factor* can result in you and your teens assuming you can read each other's minds. Your teens may become frustrated when they think you should know how they are thinking and feeling. You may become frustrated when your teens misinterpret your sarcasm.

4. **Structure and Predictability Ensure Comfort and Safety:** At a time when teens are moving toward independence, rules and consequences provide guidelines and

boundaries, which demonstrate your care and concern for your teens.

5. **A 911 Plan Ensures Safety and Security:** Create a one-word signal with your teen that she can call in or text at the time of a crisis. If your teen puts the 911 plan into action, remember to act now, ask questions later.

6. **Sometimes a Number Is Worth a Thousand Words:** A *Feeling and Action Scale* is a communication tool that can be helpful for the whole family. It allows you and your teens to communicate your feelings and helpful responses in a quick and concise manner.

CHAPTER 2

Learning How to Ask So They Want to Tell: Encouraging Your Teenagers to Want to Talk to You

As a parent of a teenager you are probably painfully aware that attempts to ask simple questions are often met with silence and anger—and sometimes even lies. You may be familiar with the frustration of a one-word response to a seemingly harmless question. It is ironic that at a time when you want nothing more than for your teenagers to feel comfortable talking to you, they are most likely to shut down.

Teenagers withdraw because they are attempting to develop their personal identities and separate from their parents. They fear that if they open up to you they will be criticized, judged, or possibly embarrassed. Your teenagers are concerned about protecting the relationships they have with you and their wish to avoid fighting with you and/or making you angry or disappointed may result in a shut down. Believe it or not, they are also afraid that what they have to say might disappoint or even bore you—hence, the common response "You wouldn't understand!"

The nature of parent–child communication is complicated for many reasons. But once you are aware of the topics that your teens are most likely to avoid—and what will make your teens shut down—you can take the next step and learn the skills that encourage your kids to want to talk.

It's Not What You Ask but How You Ask

As teens are figuring out who they are, they want to have control over not only their personal lives, but also over how and when to disclose personal information. They want to control both the type of information they reveal and when and how they reveal that information. In fact, a 2004 study published in *Communication Reports* found that teenagers are especially sensitive when adults request information in a direct manner, so the key to getting the information that you want is to be subtle and to use conversation openers. Instead of asking how the party went, for example, you may get more information by asking an indirect question such as "Were your shoes comfortable?" (No kidding!). This question about the new party shoes may lead to a discussion of how the evening went. Try the following to get your teen talking:

TRY THIS	RATHER THAN THIS
"Did you have fun?"	"Tell me all about the party."
"Would you recommend the movie you two saw?"	"Tell me everything about the date."
"Did anything funny happen today?"	"How was your day?"
"Want to see my new (handbag, tennis racket, blouse, etc)?"	"How was your day?"
"Do you need anything?"	"Why are you so upset?"
"Want to have something to eat with me?"	"Why do you seem so upset/angry?"
"Would you like a cup of tea/lemonade/glass of water?"	"What's wrong?"
"Are you happy the test is over?"	"How was the test?"
"Come sit with me."	"Come talk to me."

Remember, once you get your teens talking let them keep talking. Avoid interrupting them by asking as few questions as possible once the conversation starts flowing.

GET THEM TALKING

"I'd love your opinion on my idea."

Show that you respect your teens' opinions and they are more likely to engage you in conversation.

When using conversation openers, keep in mind that the goal is to keep your questions gentle and nonjudgmental. Always go for a soft and interested tone in your voice; loud voices beget screaming teenagers. Keep things light and you are most likely to have your child open up and let you know how things are really going. Finally, in all situations, if your teens don't want to talk, try to honor that. You will surely have many more opportunities to successfully get the conversations going.

Make Yourself Available

Your perceived availability is a major factor that predicts how likely your teens are to communicate with you. If your teens see you as being too busy to spend time with them or as simply unavailable, they are very likely to shut down. How can you find out if you're coming across as unavailable? Just ask! Parents' ratings of how available they are often differ quite a bit from their teens' ratings and you can't change anything if you don't know how they feel. If they do see you as unavailable, your goal should be to let your teens know about your availability or even to consider reexamining the amount of time you spend with them. Keep in mind that we are not suggesting that you stay home all the time hovering around your teens. We simply want you to consider spending some time at home and attempt to give your full attention to your teens if they appear to be trying to talk to you.

AND, YEAH . . . :

1. A phrase often used just as a teen is getting to the main point of a story. This phrase serves to minimize the importance of the main point of the story especially when a teen is unsure of how the story will be received.

PARENT: "Tell me more."

TEENAGER: "So I got really upset about this . . . and, yeah . . . ."

SUGGESTED PARENTAL RESPONSE: This is an opportunity to respond in an interested and neutral manner. "I am interested in the rest of the story if you feel like telling me now or later."

It can also be helpful to let your teens know that you have their well-being in mind and that you are available to listen or help. Don't ever use what your teens say against them or make it all about yourself and your own needs (e.g., "Now that I know you didn't get into that college, how will I face my friends again?").

When you are home, try to spend some time in open spaces where your teens have easy access to you and try to engage in relaxing activities such as reading, etc. Your teens are more likely to seek you out if you seem relaxed. If at all possible, try to avoid spending all of your time at home trying to meet deadlines or bringing lots of work home from the office—most teens don't feel comfortable imposing on a busy parent.

When to Avoid or Discontinue Conversations with Your Teenagers

Now that you have ideas about your role in fostering communication, we will move on to another detective skill. This involves reading your teens accurately so that you know when they clearly do not want to talk. A good detective would pick up the following cues:

- Irritability.
- Sarcasm.
- Yelling.
- Lack of eye contact.
- Changing the subject.
- Leaving the room.
- Hanging up the phone.
- One-word answers.
- Requests to delay the conversation.
- Listening but saying nothing.
- Crying.
- Slamming doors.

It is crucial for you to be sensitive to the cues that your teens offer when they do not want to answer your questions. Continued discussion in the face of these cues can result in angry, closed-off teens. At these times, you should step back and give your teens some space. Keep in mind that self-disclosure is not likely to be helpful when it is forced.

Remember, your teens are trying to gain some independence (a topic we discuss more fully in Chapter 4) and want to decide for themselves when to discuss personal information. This gives them a sense of control.

Let Them Confide in You

Now the confusing part: Although your teenagers often give you the message that they do not want to talk, they can benefit tremendously from being able to confide in you. Sharing secrets with parents has been found to reduce stress levels in teenagers and—as long as they don't feel cornered and forced into talking—opening up to you may actually make them feel better emotionally and physically. There is even evidence that self-disclosure, under the right circumstances, can actually boost the immune system. It's well known that teens who are able to confide in their parents are more likely to have high self-esteem, be free of depression, have high quality friendships, and show positive school adjustment. In addition, these teens tend to be more resilient and have an easier time dealing with the challenges of everyday life.

The best time to ensure control of and gather information about your teens is when they offer direct self-disclosure; when they feel free to open up to you on their own you'll have an effective way of learning just who they are and how they spend their time. And, when you create the right type of environment for your teens, they will want to open up to you. Also, when your teens feel able to communicate to you, they are less likely to lie. This is important for a number of reasons. How often your teens lie is related to whether and how often they will experience emotional and behavioral problems. Perhaps when teens lie, parents begin to distrust them and become less available to talk to them. This may lead to a cycle of loneliness, abandonment, and further lies. If your teens lie, you may have fewer opportunities to guide them in the right direction.

This is why it is so important for you to pay attention to your own words and actions that either encourage or discourage your teens from being open with you—especially when it comes to discussions on sex and drugs. In addition (as discussed in Chapter 1), it is how you create this environment (i.e., with you teenager's input) that can make all the difference.

Sex

Sex is a particularly sensitive topic for both parents and teens. While the majority of you understand the importance of having the initial sex talk, which provides a general overview of the birds and the bees, there are many challenges in learning how to continue this conversation. A 1998 study shows that, when talking about sex, most teens and parents report interactions which focus mainly on HIV, AIDS, and STDs. These talks are often perceived by teens as lectures. While educating teens on these sensitive topics is important, the way the information is presented can make the difference between teens listening in and tuning out. In fact, teens report that they want to discuss this topic in a mature manner. They want to be talked with—not at. In addition, they want you to listen. An interactive discussion is a must.

Teens who talk to their parents about sex are more likely to have their first sexual experience at a later age. When they are engaging in sex, they are more likely to use contraception; they are likely to have fewer partners than teens who have not talked to their parents; they are less likely to be influenced by the sexual behaviors of their peers;

and overall they are less likely to engage in risky sexual behavior. These are all important because studies have shown that many teens think they know more about sex than they actually do. For example, teens who reported that they knew all there was to know became unintentionally pregnant more often than teens who did not make this claim.

POOR EYE CONTACT:

1. An expression of embarrassment or self-consciousness.
PARENT: "That girl really seems to have a crush on you."
TEENAGER: Poor eye contact.
SUGGESTED PARENTAL RESPONSE: Drop the topic. You may have introduced an embarrassing subject.

2. A signal of lack of interest.
PARENT: "Your brother is really getting on my nerves today."
TEENAGER: Poor eye contact.
SUGGESTED PARENTAL RESPONSE: Recognize that there may be more appropriate topics of conversation and change the topic.

3. A neutral expression.
PARENT: "Want to go clothes shopping?"
TEENAGER: Poor eye contact accompanied by an emphatic "Yes."
SUGGESTED PARENTAL RESPONSE: "Wonderful, let's set up a time."

Teens who report reluctance to talk to parents about sex express several main concerns. They worry that they will feel embarrassed talking about sex, or that their parents will be embarrassed talking to them. They question their parents' knowledge about sexual behaviors. Your teens may worry about disapproval or even anger if they talk about their sexual experiences. Your teens need you to be open, supportive, and understanding. They want the opportunity to have their questions about sex answered without feeling judged. It is important that they receive the message that they can go to you without hesitation.

Early conversations about sex should focus on helping your teens and tweens understand the developmental changes they are experiencing. Your teens need you to guide them through the physical and emotional changes occurring inside so that they can learn to adapt to the social world quickly changing around them. Also, remember that discussions need to be age appropriate. For example, you may want to begin a discussion about sex with your twelve year old by focusing on the bodily changes associated with puberty. With your fifteen year old on the other hand, you can begin talking about sexual activity and pregnancy. More importantly, you need to individualize these discussions to your teens' developmental needs.

Be wary of offering conflicting messages to your teens. It is confusing, for example, to say that you expect them to abstain from sexual activity, but then to encourage them to use contraception if they *are* engaging in sexual activity. The most important rule regarding conversations about sex (or any other topic for that matter) is to listen and then respond. An open and honest approach is best. If this is a difficult topic for you to discuss with your teens, don't be afraid to let them know. Your teens are perceptive and your body language can easily give away your discomfort (see Chapter 3 for a detailed explanation on body language). A good opener may be "I am a little uncomfortable talking about this but you are important to me and I want us to try to feel comfortable discussing this." If you find yourself stuck, try some of the following examples:

TRY THIS	RATHER THAN THIS
"Now that you are getting older it's important for us to talk together about more mature topics."	"Now that you are getting older there are things I need to caution you about."
"I realize it may feel embarrassing to talk about this but I want you to know I am here to listen and answer any questions you may have."	"I would be really disappointed to find out that you are sexually active but if you are then it's important that you know all about the consequences."
"You need to know I will always be here if you need me, no matter what the situation."	"It's better to abstain so you won't get into any trouble."
Make sure that you are calm and comfortable when discussing this topic. You want your body language to suggest that you are relaxed and attentive.	Discuss the topic after you've heard some concerning information or while you are pacing or clearly anxious.

Remember, the more open and supportive you seem about discussing all sexual issues, the more your teens are likely to ask questions which may in turn help them address their own insecurities and concerns. You should try to be prepared to field *any* question once you convey that the lines of communication are unconditionally open.

Setting Boundaries

Perhaps the greatest challenge for both you and your teens is in establishing the boundaries when discussing sex. While your teens want you to respect their privacy, they welcome the opportunity to hear honest answers to difficult questions. However, you need to be wary of what you share about your own sexual experiences as well as the messages you convey with your behaviors. Parents who are perceived as sexually permissive run the risk of encouraging sexually permissive behaviors. This can be a particular challenge if you are a single parent who is dating or involved in intimate relationships. We are certainly not suggesting that you should refrain from sexual relationships, but we do want to remind you that your teens are a captive audience. Teens tend to focus on how their parents' relationships affect them and are prone to magnify *every* interaction of dating parents. In the minds of your teens simple hand holding may result in the assumption that you are having sex. Observations of your intimate interactions can result in your teens feeling angry, upset, and/or as if they are less important to you than your partner. In these situations, a direct approach is best. Talking with your teens about the nature of the relationship you have with your partner can be helpful, but *be careful.* Focus the conversation on how your relationship may impact your teens. Emphasize your love and support for them. Provide them with an opportunity to ask questions. While your answers should be honest, avoid offering unnecessary (and inappropriate) details of your relationship. Your goal is to reassure your teens that they will always be a priority, not to take them into your confidence about your love interests.

BORING:

1. A statement which conveys disinterest.

PARENT: "Isn't this show interesting?"

TEENAGER: "No, it's boring."

SUGGESTED PARENTAL RESPONSE: There is not much you can say. Remember, everyone is entitled to her opinion and this is the opinion of your teen.

2. An exclamation that infers that the teen is frustrated and therefore not listening to what is being said. It suggests "I've heard it all already."

PARENT: "You should try it this way."

TEENAGER: "Boring!"

SUGGESTED PARENTAL RESPONSE: Step back. Your teen is not ready to hear your suggestions. Revisit the topic at another time when your teen may be more receptive.

3. A statement which suggests dissatisfaction with what is being said or pointed out.

PARENT: "I'm really disappointed in you."

TEENAGER: "Boring!"

SUGGESTED PARENTAL RESPONSE: Be careful. It is easy to respond to this as an insult. Instead, offer a calm response that indicates that you will drop it for now but it may need to be revisited later. For example: "Okay, I can see that you are upset but we will need to talk about this later."

Pornography

An increasing concern for some parents is the ease with which their teens can view pornography via the Internet. Parents often ask us, "How much is too much?" and "Should I be concerned?" These are not easy questions to answer. What we do know is this: Teens who report that they seek out pornography on the Internet are also more likely to be involved in high-risk behaviors such as substance abuse. Teens who report positive relationships with their parents are less likely to engage in this behavior as are teens who report more parental supervision. Teens who view pornography are also at greater risk for depression. It is important, however, to take this information in stride. For many adolescents —especially boys—viewing pornography on the Internet decreases over time, which suggests that once the novelty wears off, many teens move on. Again, the most important thing is how you approach this topic with your teens. If open, honest, and supportive lines of communication already exist, you've already provided a forum to comfortably discuss such issues. When addressing concerns related to specific behaviors the key is to avoid encouraging embarrassment or shame. You must create a delicate balance highlighting behaviors that you find unacceptable or upsetting, while communicating support and understanding. If you are concerned that your teens are spending too much time seeking out pornography you may want to reach out to a professional.

Just Say No? Talking to Your Teens about Drugs and Understanding What They May Be Trying to Tell You

Although your kids see the ads on television and hear about substance abuse in health class, you may still wonder what they are actually learning. This is why it is important to know that the dangers of substance use (we mean alcohol too) are not communicated in one conversation. As with any high-risk behavior the more the dangers and concerns are discussed the more likely your teens are to get the message, and the less likely they are to use.

Sometimes however, the more you try to talk about drugs with your teens, the more they seem to pull away. They are especially likely to be dismissive if these discussions are perceived as hostile or demanding. This is concerning because when teens pull away, they sometimes turn to drugs to help them cope with or escape from parents they perceive as too demanding. How you approach discussing the topic with your teens will make all the difference. It is important for you to know that consistently dismissive responses—which often occur if there are certain subjects that parents do not want to discuss or are sensitive about—can put your teens at higher risk for substance abuse. Ironically substance abuse may be an attempt to get a dismissive parent's attention.

Essentially, then, the question becomes one of *how* to generate effective and informative discussions with your teens. To begin with, you better know what you're talking about! Get the facts before presenting them to your teens. Your teenagers are smart and with the availability of the Internet they have direct access to the facts. They also have access to a lot of conflicting, contradictory, and incorrect information that may confuse or mislead them. Your teens want to be treated as intelligent individuals and a fact-based approach in presenting information to your teens suggests that they are in control. It is important that you trust that given accurate information your teens will make informed decisions.

A good strategy when discussing drugs is to capitalize on any relevant opportunities that present themselves. This can be as easy as suggesting your teens read an article in the morning paper. Make sure, however, to discuss and translate the article. Nothing is more frustrating than reading something that you are supposed to understand but can't. If the article uses jargon or technical terms restate the content in a clearer manner so that you don't embarrass your teens. If the article talks about the side effects of a specific drug, you could restate this more simply by saying: "So isn't this interesting that they found that some of the unexpected things that can happen when you take this drug are . . . ." Another opportunity may arise when your teens tell you about a situation related to their peers. If they tell you about a party that got broken up by the police due to noise and or/underage drinking, then use that opportunity to begin a conversation. Other conversation starters include the following:

TRY THIS	RATHER THAN THIS
"What do you think about what some of the other parents are saying about drug use at the high school?" If your teen refuses to talk, ask the following "What time would be a good time for us to sit down together? I really need your perspective on this. I'll make the tea."	"I need to explain to you why I am concerned about substance use."
"I found an interesting article in the paper today. I am curious what you think."	"This article says XYZ, you need to read it."
"What do you think about that situation with Terry?"	"I hope that situation with Terry teaches you a lesson."
"What did you think about that movie/show about XYZ (where XYZ represents a situation where using drugs or alcohol resulted in a negative situation for the protagonist) last night?"	"I hope that movie/show about XYZ last night taught you a lesson."

WHY?

1. A question that indicates that your teen doubts and/or disagrees with you.

PARENT: "You have to go to her party."

TEENAGER: "Why?"

SUGGESTED PARENTAL RESPONSE: Ask your teen if she wants to hear your reasons. If not, let it go for another time.

2. A question that suggests that your teen is making an honest inquiry.

PARENT: "We have to find out about that."

TEENAGER: "Why?"

SUGGESTED PARENTAL RESPONSE: Offer a complete and honest explanation.

Home Supervision

We all know about the cool parents. You know, the ones who let their underage teens drink or smoke under their supervision in the home. Not surprisingly, teens who have parents who permit such behaviors are more likely to engage in these behaviors both at earlier ages and more frequently both inside and outside of their homes than teens whose parents do not allow these behaviors. In fact, teens whose parents have firm rules about substance use tend to drink/use at later ages (or not at all) and have lower consumption rates than their peers. Both studies and our own clinical experience have shown us that when it comes to drugs, when parents give an inch and allow marijuana or alcohol use teens often take a yard and frequently and heavily consume these substances and/or move on to more hard-core substances.

Is Honesty the Best Policy? Answering Your Teens If They Ask about Your Substance Use History

As we already alluded to in our discussion on sex, you need to be wary of the message your own behavior communicates to your teens. We are sure that you do not need us to tell you that talking about the perils of drinking with a martini in your hand does not make a convincing argument. In general, teens whose parents have a history of substance use are at higher risk to use than teens whose parents do not have such a history. The explanations for this finding vary and include genetic predisposition for addiction to substances, parent modeling behavior, and permissive or neglectful parenting due to parents' own substance involvements. Little has been studied regarding parents' past occasional or recreational use. One question we often hear from parents is "What should I tell my teens when they ask about my past experiences with substances?" If you have no history of using substances before adulthood (including tobacco and alcohol) then you can say something like, "I know you are aware that I have a glass of wine with dinner. When you are an adult you'll have the opportunity to make informed decisions for yourself" and skip on to the next section. For those of you still with us, the answer is tricky.

As we have reinforced throughout this book, difficult topics should always be presented in the form of an interactive discussion. While it is important to be honest with your teens, use your judgment. If you have used extensively in the past, there may be no reason to offer a detailed account of everything you used and how much. Take the opportunity to teach, discuss, and learn from your teens. Present the context in which you used and highlight any resulting consequences and/or regrets. Be responsive to additional questions and be sure to explain why you no longer engage in these behaviors. Convey your own concerns regarding your teens' engaging in these behaviors. In the end, as we have said over and over (and will continue to reinforce throughout this book) open and ongoing communication with your kids will result in teens who are happier and healthier.

Translating Behavior: The Signs That Your Teens May Be Using Drugs

It doesn't take a psychologist to realize that if your teens are coming home intoxicated or high they are telling you that they may have a problem. The more common question parents ponder is "How many times is too many?" While there really is no magic number frequency should be taken into account. Episodes of substance use should be examined in the context of the other signs of use and abuse. Below we present lists of obvious and not so obvious indicators that your teens may be using. We caution that it is important to take these signs in the context of how your teen generally behaves. You should also realize that we present these lists as guidelines. Just because your teens may be exhibiting some of these behaviors does not mean they are using. What you should be looking for are noticeable changes in their previous behavior patterns.

OBVIOUS INDICATORS OF SUBSTANCE USE

- Coming home intoxicated or high.
- Scent of substance (e.g., alcohol or marijuana) on breath and/or clothes.
- Changes in appearance (e.g., wearing the same clothes for days or looking disheveled and unkempt).
- Changes in attitude or behaviors (e.g., increased agitation or irritability or social isolation especially at home).

SUBTLE INDICATORS OF SUBSTANCE USE

- Changes in sleep patterns.
- Changes in appetite.
- Changes in peer group; failure to introduce new friends.
- Decline in academic performance.
- Loss of interest/involvement in previously enjoyed activities.
- Increased requests for money.
- Missing money and/or valuable objects.
- Lying.

I Know My Teen Is Using Drugs. How Should This Be Addressed?

Okay, so maybe you put the pieces of the puzzle together and the picture is clear—your teen has a problem. Or, maybe an event or situation has resulted in this conclusion about your adolescent. Perhaps you are at a loss about what to do or say to your teen. Good news. We are not.

To begin with, you need to discuss this sensitive issue with your teens when they are in a state that encourages conversation. Do not discuss your teens' substance use when they are drunk or high. While they may *seem* sober enough to have the conversation, this opens the door for them to deny that such a conversation ever took place. On a good day, they may report that they remember having the conversation but cannot remember the content. This is a serious issue and you do not want to provide opportunities to *not* be heard.

When you do address the issue make sure you remain as calm as possible. Even a slight modulation in either your vocal rate or tone can result in an automatic turn-off switch in your teens' attentiveness. It is important to come across as nonthreatening yet concerned. If you have a partner, you may want to decide ahead of time who is better equipped to discuss this issue—less emotion is better.

When trying to determine the extent of your teens' use and/or gather other related facts, it is best to ask open-ended questions. For example: "So how many times a week have you been smoking pot?" We can assure you if during this information seeking session you happen to make an inaccurate assumption, your teen's reaction will immediately clarify this for you. We caution, however, that teens who have perfected the art of lying may be able to feign an untruthful response. In response to the question asked above, for example, an untruthful teen could respond: "What are you talking about? I cannot believe you think I would do that!" Do not let his emotional response move you. It is important to calmly continue with your questions. If you have definite facts that counter your teen's claims, gently advise him. Continuing with the interchange highlighted above for example: "I understand that you may feel embarrassed or ashamed that we have found out about this, but we know this is true. I'd rather discuss how we can work together on this rather than argue over facts."

Offer to find help without being judgmental. It is important however to acknowledge that this is not a problem that will resolve itself, no matter how convincing your teens seem to be when they say they can quit on their own. We understand how much you want to believe this, but minimizing or denying the problem will ensure that it will not only continue but could possibly get worse. The quicker your teens get treatment the better chance they have of recovering. If you're still not sure how to handle this situation, try the following:

TRY THIS	RATHER THAN THIS
Sit down with your teens and calmly discuss your concerns about their substance use when they are sober.	Discuss or yell at your teens when they come home under the influence.
"So you're using every day?"	"Are you using drugs? How often?"
In the face of denial: "I know this is hard to discuss, we are not asking you whether you are using, we are asking how we can help you to stop using."	"Stop lying, we know you are using." Or (with real facts in hand in response to your teen's denial) "I am sorry, what a relief. I believe you that you are not using."
"Let's research treatment options together and discuss which one would be best for you."	"We are so glad you are going to stop on your own."

Social Networking

You walk into your family room where your teen is quickly pecking away at the computer keyboard. You look over her shoulder to quickly scan the content of the IM she is currently writing. You act disinterested but the truth is, you are really confused. What the heck does "P911, P.O.S." mean? Is that even English? You're upset because you're doing exactly what all the experts have told you to—monitoring your teen's Internet use—but is this really doing anything when she's not even conversing in a language you understand? As parents have become more astute about monitoring their teenagers' Internet use, teens have responded by creating a language of abbreviations so they can continue to protect their privacy. So, what do you need to know? First that technology is here to stay. So let's focus on how to deal with it.

GET THEM TALKING

"Come have some cookies with me."
Being available and having your teens be with you physically increases the likelihood that they will talk to you.

Beyond Computer 101

We know we don't have to remind you that your teens should not be allowed to have computers in their rooms; instead keep them in more public spaces in your home. This location encourages your teens to be more mindful about what they are looking at and chatting about on the Internet. It has also been found that parents tend to monitor what their teens are doing online more vigilantly when computers are in common household spaces.

But despite this, there has been a great shift in how teens are using the Internet these days and, as technologies have advanced, the doorway for social networking has opened wider and wider. While much of what we focus on in this book is related to *what* teenagers are communicating, we would be remiss if we did not at least explore *how* (specifically by what technological mechanisms) they are communicating.

Over the past decade as the Internet has become more universal, both parents and teens have become wiser about its use. But while your teens are certainly acting wiser in many respects on the Internet, concerns still exist. When parents in one survey were asked to look at their children's online profiles, almost 80% reported that they were concerned about what they saw. They reported that they questioned the appropriateness of at least some of the content. Toward that end, a portion of teens acknowledge that they post a fake age online. Of some concern is that a vast majority also post videos and photos to which they allow public access (meaning anyone can view them). Even more concerning is that nearly half of all teens do not acknowledge any personal risk in making these postings. A majority of teens surveyed have even indicated that they have posted the towns in which they live and/ or their schools' names on public access sites.

So while teens may have become more Internet savvy, many teens who report that their parents have not talked to them about Internet safety report higher risk behavior. Studies have shown that teens who do not communicate that often with their parents or who have conflicting relationships with their parents are more likely to form intimate online relationships. Teens already engaging in other high-risk behaviors are also more likely to form such online bonds. These "friendships" may be with unsafe individuals misrepresenting who they are and what they are about.

HEAD NODDING:

1. An attempt to dismiss you and tune you out.

PARENT: "You really should start to do your homework."

TEENAGER: Nods head.

SUGGESTED PARENTAL RESPONSE: No need to repeat yourself and be labeled a nag. Just simply say "I think that would help with time management." If you feel dismissed, gently reinforce your original statement without becoming repetitive.

2. An expression of true agreement.

PARENT: "Your friend Kate seems very nice."

TEENAGER: Nods head.

SUGGESTED PARENTAL RESPONSE: None. Just be happy. You two are in agreement!

3. An expression of uncertainty about how to respond.

PARENT: "I hate my boss."

TEENAGER: Nods head.

SUGGESTED PARENTAL RESPONSE: Drop the topic. Perhaps your teen doesn't know how to respond.

What Do They Know?

Today's teens have been born into a world of technology. Much like children raised in bilingual homes are easily fluent in two languages, your teens are able to comprehend how to use the tools of technology easily because they have been exposed to them since birth. While some of you are probably just as savvy as your teens in navigating these social networking sites (such as MySpace, Facebook, and Twitter), for many adults they are a struggle to understand, let alone keep up with. Below you will find a list of questions we recommend that you ask your teens regarding the sites they are accessing in order to help you understand what they are doing and on what type of sites:

- "What is the site used for?"
- "Who has access to the information you post?"
- "How do you set the privacy settings (if applicable)?"
- "When/what do you post?"
- "How can I access what you have posted?"

We could not casually slip in the last question in our list without offering a brief explanation. The discussion between parents and teens regarding access to their social network postings (online profiles, journals, blogs, collections of photos, and/or videos) can be a heated one. It is, however, worth having this discussion. If you opt not to check what your teens are posting in order to allow them to maintain their privacy, make sure you consider this decision carefully. After all, since when is the world wide web private? If you accidentally find a secret journal under the mattress when you are making your daughter's bed, that's private and should not be read. A publically accessible online journal or blog entry, however, is far from private! While your teens may object to your having access to their postings, the very nature of posting content online is to allow a large number of people access. As a parent you need to ask yourself, "Why doesn't she want me to have access?" We know that teens argue in the name of privacy, but, in fact, teens who believe their parents are fully monitoring their Internet activities report they are less likely to engage in behaviors that they believe their parents would not approve such as posting inappropriate or provocative content.

GET THEM TALKING

"I'm proud of the way you handled that."

When they feel praised, they are more likely to engage you in conversation.

We encourage you to request a demonstration of how sites are used. This will send a message to your teens that you are not only interested in learning about *what* they are doing, but also want to be kept aware of *how*. Tutorials from your teens may also allow you to learn how to access social networking tools that you may find useful. You can provide a wonderful opportunity for your teens to feel empowered and competent by requesting their aid in introducing you to these new tools. If you would like to set up your own profile on a social networking site or become a blogger, invite your teens to help you. There are many benefits to this experience. By affording your teens the opportunity to teach you, you send the message that you value their skills and knowledge. Use the experience as an invitation to demonstrate gratitude and appreciation to your teens. These positive feelings go a long way in strengthening the bond in any relationship.

Your Teens May Be on Their Best Behavior, but Are You?

We suggest you gain access to your teens' sites by requesting their user names and passwords. Keep in mind, if you decide to monitor your teens by "friending" them on a social networking site, you are offering them access to your postings as well. Be careful what you post, remember your teens are watching!

Also, be upfront about your plans to monitor your teens' sites. At all costs, do *not* attempt to be deceptive—this usually leads to unnecessary drama and conflict. Confronting your teens about inappropriate content will be difficult and we can assure you that they will want to focus on your deception, not on the inappropriate content. However, if your teens are aware that you are monitoring their sites, then you can address the issues directly.

If There Is a Will There Is a Way

Even if you have made the decision to actively monitor your teens' social networking pages, there are ways your teens can still hide postings from you. One method is to set up more than one profile page on a social networking site. This way, teens can carefully manage the pages you see. Be careful how you decide to monitor the sites used by your teens. As always an interactive discussion about how and why you plan to monitor these sites is usually most effective. Let your teens know that you are aware that kids sometimes have multiple profiles in an effort to avoid monitoring. Explain to them why this would concern you.

In addition, it's important to clarify that your intent is not to get involved with their social networking activities; it is simply to monitor content. After checking the content on your teens' sites and pages, do not then try to engage them in conversation about what you read unless it is to discuss inappropriate or concerning content. Such a discussion may anger your teens and make them feel as if you are monitoring their sites to invade their privacy. If you are interested in what is going on in your teens' social life, engage them in a discussion. Let them know you will assume they are being upfront with you about the sites they use and the pages they maintain. In an interactive discussion, develop rules and consequences regarding your access to their sites.

Gaming

In recent years, gaming has become another popular teen activity. This is especially true for boys although girls are catching up. What is of great concern is that a majority of parents report that they have never stopped their teen from buying a video game because of the rating. Perhaps even more concerning is that a large portion of parents admit they do not completely understand the ESRB rating system (the system which assigns the ratings). A 2005 study showed that teenagers who watch violent television and play violent video games are more aggressive than teens who do not. In addition, these teens view the world as more hostile and negative than do their peers.

Here are the gaming guidelines we suggest:

TRY THIS	RATHER THAN THIS
"So what do you know about how you play this game and what it is about? I thought I heard that this happened." (Describe what you know.)	"I heard this is a very violent game which I do not believe is appropriate because . . . ."
"Why do you think a parent may be concerned about the content?"	"The content is too violent for you."
Have a discussion before your teen buys/plays the game.	Tell your teen he can't buy/play after he has already done so.
If you are okay with some play: "Let's come up with some guidelines about when and for how long you can play." Or if you are not okay with the content: "I understand that you think you would enjoy this game but I am not comfortable with you buying/playing it because of the content we discussed. Let's see if there is another game we can both agree on that would be appropriate for you to play."	"Under no circumstances can you play/buy this game and that is final."

Was There Life Before Cell Phones?

Cell phone and computer technology has evolved so quickly that those seeking to understand the who, what, and why are having difficulty keeping up with the advances. The latest generation of cell phones with Internet capability allows texts and IMs to be received and responded to in real time. How wonderful, right? Well, maybe not. Now your teens have to deal with new types of peer pressure and develop new coping skills in order to manage them.

The Pressure of Keeping Up with the Demand

Because teens don't go anywhere without their cell phones these days—incidentally, do you?—they often feel compelled to immediately respond to every text message and instant message they receive. They fear they may miss out on something important or possibly alienate or anger one of their friends. If they can't or don't want to respond, they may claim poor cell coverage or post *away messages* (messages which explain why they are not available). You can help your teens cope by imposing times at which their phones must be turned off. In extreme cases where your teens have difficulty complying with this rule—especially at night, for example—we recommend that you take custody of their phones to ensure compliance.

The Pressure of the List

The list of friends that teens have on their cell phones and social networking pages has become a status symbol for teens. It is all about *who* (the names) and *how many* (the number of names) are on the list. Chances are however that your teens rarely, if ever, communicate with more than half of the friends on their lists. If they want to avoid interacting with someone on their list, most teens use blocking, which prevents others from seeing that they are online. In addition, although your teens generally feel compelled to respond when they receive a message, most teens report they simply ignore messages from people with whom they do not want to talk with, especially if they feel someone is being intrusive.

The Language of Communication

Texting and IMing via cell phone have also resulted in a new kind of freedom and feeling of independence for teens. This is especially true for teens who are not yet driving. It allows them to be in control by providing them the opportunity to coordinate activities directly with their friends in real time. Although Sydney's dad may be driving them to the movies, Sydney can silently text Amanda and let her know how far away they are from her house. Teen independence is further reinforced because teens can communicate with each other without the awareness of the adults in their lives.

In order to save time while utilizing these new real-time communication tools, a new language continues to evolve at a rapid pace. This means that understanding how the technology works is not enough to help you monitor your teens. Below we present a small sampling (and we mean small) of some commonly used abbreviations and translations that will help keep you in the know.

ABBREVIATION	DEFINITION
9	Parent is watching.
99	Parent is no longer watching.
P911	Parent alert.
PA	Parent alert.
PAL	Parents are listening.
PAW	Parents are watching.
PBB	Parents are behind back.
POM	Parents over my shoulder.
POS	Parents over my shoulder.

ABBREVIATION	DEFINITION
CD9	Code 9-Parents around.
KPC	Keeping parents clueless.
A/S/L/P	Age/Sex/Location/Picture.
RU/18	Are you over 18?
DOC	Drug of choice.
EWI	E-mailing while intoxicated.
FUBAR/FUBB	F***ed up beyond recognition/F***ed up beyond belief.
IGHT	I got high tonight.
420	Marijuana use or sometimes "let's get high."
LIK	Liquor.
MUBAR	Messed up beyond recognition.

Thankfully the Internet not only houses a forum for conversing in this language (via IM) but also interactive dictionary websites such as *www.webopedia.com* that can keep you up to date on all the abbreviations used in conversation. We highly recommend that you check this site out or any one of a number of additional translation websites to become more fluent.

Parenting via Cell Phone

It is difficult to recall a time when cell phones did not exist. Not long ago, mobile phone use was considered an exclusive luxury. Over the past twenty years mobile phone use has gone from exclusive to common to necessary. How did parents monitor their kids before the use of cell phones? Was there a life before texting? It is hard to remember. While cell phones have become the main source of teens' real-time communication, parents have reaped the benefits as well. As a result of cell phone technology you can now contact your teens on a moment's notice. A quick text back and forth can identify where your teens are located and with whom. Simple questions such as "What do you want for dinner?" or "When are you coming home?" can be delivered instantaneously. Mandates such as "Be home by 5 P.M." or requests such as "Please stop at the store and get a gallon of milk." have made life seemingly simpler. This ability to contact teens immediately has resulted in more confidence and fewer concerns. Of course there are a few concerns that you must consider and with which you must sometimes contend and we would be remiss not to highlight these issues.

Cell phone responses offer false security. Just because your teen calls or texts where and with whom they are, does not mean they are telling the truth. This behavior has resulted in parents making more attempts to monitor their teens' behaviors in ways other than texting or calling. Our experience is that sometimes parents have become so reliant on cell phone calls that they have inadvertently become permissive in their parenting style. If you have concerns regarding the validity of your teens' whereabouts, let technology work in your favor. Have your teens call from a land line if possible. If you have caller ID, and your teens are not calling from restricted numbers, you will be able to verify their locations. Although many mobile phones now even have GPS capability, it's always best to parent the way you would if cell phones did not exist. If your teens, for example, tell you they are at a supervised friend's home, request to speak with the adult in charge. If you are truly concerned, and are particularly technology savvy, have your teen send a photo or live video stream of where he is and who he is with. We realize this may sound extreme but not only will it answer your concerns, it will send the message that you care about his safety and that you are aware that there are ways in which you can be deceived. If your teens have a history of misreporting where they are, work with them on rules and consequences (see Chapter 1) to address this concern.

To Read or Not to Read, the Temptation of the Text

You walk into your kitchen one day and notice your daughter's shiny pink cell phone sitting on the counter. You feel as if it is calling to you "Read my texts, check my ingoing and outgoing messages and phone numbers." Our advice: *Stop* right there. As a parent, you certainly have the authority to require your teens to disclose how they are using their cell phones. This is true regardless of whether you or your teens are paying the bills. However, sneaking and peeking is not the way to gather this information.

Many parents report they have mixed feelings about whether they should be checking their teens' cell phones. They justify peaking with the excuse that as long as they don't read anything concerning, they will feel more confident about deciding not to check. This indirect approach, however, can equal trouble. Teens tend to keep pretty good track of their social affairs and social networking devices. We can recall more than a few times when our work involved helping parents and teens repair relationships broken due to a parent's misstep or misread. Specifically, parents who have read their teens' texts have mistakenly discussed the information with their teens acting as though their teens had actually volunteered that information. Their teens in turn became angry and shut down because they realized that the only way their parents could possess that knowledge was as a result of having looked in their cell phones. On other occasions, parents have read inappropriate or concerning texts by sneaking a peak. When they went to confront their teens about this concerning behavior, their teens were focused solely on the breach of trust and not on their parents' concerns. The bottom line is this: if you intend to check your teens' cell phone activity, you need to be upfront and honest about how you will be doing this. As always this should involve an interactive discussion with your teens. If your teens protest, take the opportunity to emphasize that if there is nothing concerning revealed, then there is no reason for them to be concerned. Enlist your teens' help in devising a supervision plan. Decide, for example, if you will check their information by randomly asking to see their phones, or will you be checking the numbers and texts by contacting your service carrier; this information is readily and easily accessed by parents via computer. If you are checking content, will you routinely discuss what you read or will you agree only to discuss concerning information? For example, if your teen is engaging in inappropriate cell phone use by *sexting* (sending sexually explicit texts, photos, or videos via cell phone—see Chapter 4) it is important that you can address this directly and carefully. If you decide to check by looking at your teens' cell phone, remember they can easily delete any information they do not want you to see. It is for this reason that we recommend the carrier option to parents with concerns.

You may feel like you have been presented with an impossible task! You need to get your teenagers to talk to you in the face of a high level of resistance. We hope that as you complete this chapter you feel more confident in your abilities to understand what your teens are telling you verbally. In the next chapter we offer insight regarding how to read what they are saying nonverbally through their body language and behaviors.

1. **Avoid the Trap of Asking Too Many Questions:** Allow your teens to set the pace of disclosure. Let them volunteer information. If you ask too many questions you are likely to get short answers, unreliable information, and to be rejected.

2. **Provide Opportunities for Disclosure:** As you already know, teenagers will leak information in the most unexpected ways. It is important that you spend unpressured time with your teens so that they have opportunities to share information and/or think out loud.

3. **Try Hard Not to Criticize, Judge, or Become Angry:** When given information, try hard to just listen. By providing a nonjudgmental and supportive forum for your teens, you encourage them to honestly discuss their questions and concerns.

4. **Talk with Your Teens, Not at Them:** By treating your teens maturely you communicate confidence in their ability to discuss sensitive topics. Avoid embarrassing or shaming your teens when discussing issues of concern.

5. **Communication Equals Prevention:** Teens whose parents communicate openly with them are less likely to engage in high-risk behaviors.

6. **Be Aware:** It is important to be cognizant of the obvious and not-so-obvious signs that may indicate that your teens are engaging in high-risk behaviors.

7. **Tune In:** In order to be in tune with your teens you need to tune up your knowledge of the technology and language they utilize and keep up as these continue to evolve.

8. **New Technology, New Social Pressures:** Talk to your teens about the social pressures brought on by immediate access to technology. Help them to develop strategies to manage.

CHAPTER 3

Translating Nonverbal Communication: When Silence Speaks Volumes

There is yet another type of language that our teenagers speak and that is body language. While words are used mainly to convey information, body language, if read correctly, can also convey strong messages without the need to speak. Teenagers may be reluctant to open up and share, but their thoughts and feelings may still be revealed through their body language. In fact, one of the best ways to understand your teenagers may be to pay attention to their body language and nonverbal behaviors. In effect, it is often the things they are not saying to you verbally that hold the most meaning. But how do you figure out what they are really trying to say if they aren't saying it directly? Our hope is that as you read through the pages of this chapter, the answers to that question will become evident.

Know What You're Looking For

Simply put, body language (i.e., nonverbal communication) is communication without the use of words. It is an outward reflection of a person's attitude or emotional state. Body language accounts for a significant amount of meaningful communication and is most effective when verbal and nonverbal messages appear to be in agreement. However, nonverbal signals may carry more impact than the spoken word so, when the two appear to be out of sync, we may dismiss the words and rely on the nonverbal messages. Your teenagers may be reluctant to share their thoughts and feelings with you, but they speak volumes via their body language nonetheless. The key, then, is to pay attention and know what the signs are that you are looking for. Becoming an accurate body-language reader will take time and practice. Hang in there; it will reap major rewards. You will begin to read your teens more accurately and you actually may come to be seen as an attuned parent who gets it.

In the interest of making you an expert reader of your teenagers' nonverbal behaviors, here are some of their most common types of body language and what they are likely to imply.

- *Hanging around you, but not initiating conversation.* This may mean that your teens want to spend time with you but are having a hard time saying it directly. Take a risk and suggest that you and your teens get involved in an activity together. This may be as simple as taking a walk.
- *Placing the fingers or hand on the mouth while telling you a story.* The act of mouth covering may be a signal that your teens are telling a lie. Simply ask your teens if that's really the whole story. Ask once only. If your teens say "Yes" you will be attempting to engage in "verbal overkill" if you ask repeatedly. This is a guaranteed conversation killer.
- *Poor eye contact.* They lack the confidence to look you in the eye. Remember, these are self-conscious teenagers. If your teens have trouble making eye contact with you, involve them in an activity where you can talk, but not necessarily face to face. Walking is

a good suggestion. If you walk side by side you can talk without the pressure of sustained eye contact.

- *Fist-clenched, arms-crossed.* Your teens are feeling angry and defensive. Give your teens some alone time, also known as cooling down time. They will appreciate it. Take your teens seriously, let them have their space and, above all, let them know that you are available later if they want to talk.

- *Slouching body posture.* There are a few possibilities here. Your teens could either be unhappy and stressed, feeling a bit down, or feeling good but lost in thought. Make yourself available, but don't hover. By all means do not tell your teens to sit up or stand up straight. This is not the time for concerns about posture.

- *A smile that involves the mouth and muscles around the eyes.* Your teens are truly pleased. Enjoy the moment and consider smiling yourself!

- *Your teen is looking at you, but her body and feet are pointed away from you.* The direction in which your daughter's body is directed is where she would like to be going. Perhaps it is time to end the conversation and return to it at another time. Allow her to move on and you can do the same.

- *Synchronous body language.* You and your teens seem to be matching each others' expressions and nonverbal behaviors. You two are in sync. You are probably engaging in a mutually positive conversation. Enjoy it! Learn from it!

- *Head nodding, and other noninterruptive comments such as "uh-huh," "hmmm," or "right" (without sarcastic tone).* Your teens may be indicating agreement and acceptance of the conversation. Carry on with the conversation. They may actually be listening.

- *Your teen is standing closer to you than usual when involved in a conversation and is using a pleasant tone of voice.* Your teen is probably feeling emotionally close to you. Again, carry on with the conversation. Your teen is possibly enjoying the conversation.
- *Smirk.* Each side of the face shows a different emotion. This sends the message of sarcasm. End the conversation; it's obviously not genuine.
- *Repetitive leg or foot shaking.* Your teens are uncomfortable and would like to escape the situation. It's probably time to terminate the conversation. Perhaps, you can return to it in another manner, at another time.

It's important to keep in mind that different motions may mean different things at different times. Crossed arms during a conversation may mean something entirely different than when one is very cold and trying to warm up. If your teens enter your personal space when they are angry it probably means something entirely different than if they enter your personal space if they are feeling close to you. Remember the rule that body language should be considered in context.

Distress Signals

Most parents struggle with their reactions to their teenager's body language. This is because they are struggling to familiarize themselves with a whole set of social signals. The good news is that as you get to know your son's personality, he will likely steer you in the right direction—especially when it comes to providing you with distress signals. When observing any of the signals below consider ways of helping him. Give him the choice of talking to you or to a professional. Depending on the severity and number of signals present, a professional evaluation for depression, substance abuse, etc., may be helpful.

- **Sad Smiles, Glum Faces:** A formerly happy teen begins to look glum, even sad in school, with friends, and at home. As the adage goes, "A picture is worth a thousand words." Some facial expressions are easy to detect, but others often go unnoticed. Smiles that involve the lips and the muscles around the eyes are usually true smiles. Smiles that involve the lips only without any movement around the eyes may be an attempt to fake happiness. This teen may be somewhat depressed.

- **Shallow Breathing, Shakiness, Difficulty Focusing:** Your teen may be experiencing an increase in stress in her life and may be having difficulty managing it. She may feel pressured by schoolwork, friendship issues, and/or family difficulties. These signs may indicate that she is experiencing anxiety.

- **Teen Begins to Suddenly Ignore and Avoid You:** Teens who formerly made some contact with you, now leave the room when you enter, make less eye contact, and always seem to keep you at a distance. Perhaps your teens are harboring a secret and/or are ashamed and embarrassed about something. Your teens may be afraid that you will get angry if they open up to you.

- **Nostril-Flaring, Shaking the Head from Side to Side, and Perhaps Even Mimicking Your Stance:** This is not a good cluster of behaviors. Yikes! Something has gone very wrong here. Perhaps your teens feel that you are clueless and don't get it or they are feeling put down. There are other possible scenarios here. Your teens may be angry and frustrated in the moment and have decided to make you the target. If you feel that this may be the case try not to aggravate the situation any further.

GET THEM TALKING

"How did the weather affect your plans?"
You can expect an answer about the weather and then a discussion about the day.

Again, if you are trying to get your teenagers to talk to you about the distress signals noted above refer to Chapter 2, and if you experience a lack of success you should consider a professional assessment.

Your Nonverbal Behavior

While we are on the subject of teen body language, it is essential that you remember to attend to your own nonverbal behavior. Unknowingly and unintentionally, parents often send signals that get their teens to shut down. An unwelcome nonverbal response can instantly turn your talkative teens into quiet and angry ones. You may be left baffled, when in the midst of a conversation your teens suddenly end the dialogue. What you don't realize is that you, in fact, have flipped the switch that turned off the dialogue.

Above all, no matter the topic, it is crucial to *not* give your teens the message that you are shocked, alarmed, disgusted, and/or totally distraught by what they are telling you. Although you may, in fact, be having these feelings, practice managing them. Your teens have gathered up the courage to open up to you and are probably already very concerned about your reaction. They are trusting you with their stories and are likely to be overwhelmed by their emotions; they are hoping to get comfort and support. The minute they sense intense emotion from you, you will lose them. They watch you very carefully, although it may not be apparent.

GET THEM TALKING --------------------------------------

"You worked hard, I'm sorry it was such a hard test."

If you start with praise then you can expect more of a response.

Facial Expressions

A 2008 study published in the *Journal of Nonverbal Behavior* found that as children develop into teenagers they read more negative meaning and anger into facial expressions. This translates into your teens seeing you as perhaps angrier than you actually are and reading nonverbal rejection into your neutral or only slightly negative, facial expressions. This is because as kids get older they begin to understand that people sometimes hide negative emotions. Therefore, your teens expect that you, to some extent, are holding back your true emotions. It follows that they are likely to suspect that you are hiding your true emotions more than you actually are. This may explain why a simple glance at your teen may result in your teen screaming, "Why are you glaring at me? I didn't do anything wrong." The bottom line is that your teens are not only sensitive to your nonverbal messages but, in fact, they may overreact to neutral or slightly negative body language. Therefore, effective communication with your teens is more likely when you keep your nonverbal cues balanced and in check.

GET THEM TALKING

"I'm proud of the way you handled that."
When your teens feel praised, they are more likely to engage you in conversation.

Other Nonverbal Cues

Not only are your teens reading your facial expressions, but they are also attending to other less obvious nonverbal cues—such as body movements, tone of voice, and quick shifts in mood—that may also influence their decisions to talk or not to talk. Your teens believe that they can't always take you at face value so they will search for other less obvious body cues including but not limited to pulling away, tensing the body, and avoiding eye contact. Obviously, they may or may not always be correct in their interpretations, but the important message is that they will try to read you for any sign of negativity before deciding whether or not to confide in you. Remember they don't want to upset or disappoint you. Below we provide you with a guide to helpful and not-so-helpful nonverbal signals to help you encourage your teens to talk:

TRY THIS	RATHER THAN THIS
Nod your head occasionally.	Stare blankly at your teens.
Orient your body toward your teens.	Move in a different direction. Give the impression that you would rather be anywhere else.
Smile.	Look away, avert your gaze, and make it clear that you have lost interest.
Maintain a calm and even tone of voice.	Clench your fists, grit your teeth, and narrow your eyes so your intense emotions are clearly visible.
Use occasional displays of affection such as patting on the back or lightly touching the shoulder.	Use any opportunity to escape. Answer the phone, check your texts, or tend to the dog. Indicate clearly that you have more important things to do.

Despite the do's and don'ts offered in the table above your teens may still misinterpret your body language. If you sense that this is happening try to turn the misunderstanding into an opportunity to talk. Some suggestions for giving you and your teens a second chance include the following.

- Ask your teen if you can try again and use a calm tone of voice.
- Ask your teen if you've come across angry and reassure him that you are not.
- "Did I upset you?" is always a nonthreatening, nonblaming question.
- "Can we take a break and talk when you are ready to?"

- "I am really happy to talk to you. Sorry if I give you the wrong impression."
- "I may seem distracted, but I am really not. I am very interested in your opinions."
- "Please forgive me if I seemed upset. I have a lot on my mind. Nothing, though, is more important to me than talking to you."
- "You know that I sometimes come across as nervous when I'm actually excited. Let's keep talking."
- "I didn't mean to be judgmental if that's what you thought. I'm just trying to listen to you without interrupting."

What all of these second-chance requests have in common is reassurance. You are attempting to reassure your teens that you are listening to them and are not upset with them. Do this in a private spot and do your best to appear calm, attentive, relaxed, and neutral. This is the recipe for successful dialogue. Your goal is to be a person to whom your teens can come to to get things "off their chests."

Your own feelings about the discussion should be thought about and/or discussed with a confidante. Do not use your teens as a sounding board. Of course, once you have had several hours to consider what your teens have told you, you will have to decide if the situations require any action or attention. If you decide to take action, remember to involve your teens. If you have an idea for them, share it with gentle suggestions. You want to give your teens the impression that you believe in them and that you are simply suggesting ideas that they may want to consider.

Understanding Outward Appearance—When and When Not to Worry

Through the way they look, teenagers communicate not only a desire to fit in with their peers but also a desire to gain some independence from their parents. Teenagers try on many new things including new personalities and new clothing; sometimes, the new clothing is to complement the new personality. At the same time, adolescents face a quandary as there is a great deal of value placed on dress conformity. Interestingly, clothing choice is one of the main reasons teenagers are teased. Imagine trying to fit in in exactly the right sort of way!

HANGING AROUND YOU QUIETLY:

1. A signal that emotional support is needed.

PARENT: "Anything you want to tell me?"

TEENAGER: Continues to say nothing, but seems to be spending time at your side.

SUGGESTED PARENTAL RESPONSE: None. Respect your teen's quiet desire to be near you. There's no need to apply pressure and possibly have your teen avoid you completely. She'll talk when she's ready.

2. A signal that your teen enjoys your company.

PARENT: "Do you need something?"

TEENAGER: Continues to quietly hang around you.

SUGGESTED PARENTAL RESPONSE: None. Be pleased that your teen wants to be in your company.

Understandably, you may become distressed at some of your teen's clothing choices. Hold back the urge to scream *"What do you think you are wearing?"* In most cases, clothing choice represents nothing more than an attempt to communicate, "I am a teenager now and I'd like to fit in with my peer group." Every stage in life requires a way of dressing and adolescence is no different. Unfortunately, the requirements of teenage dress do not always involve styles that are pleasing to parents (think back to what your parents may have said about what you were wearing!). While exploring how to respond to your teenager's dress and physical appearance you should always keep in mind how closely linked these factors are with self-development and social acceptance.

When you do decide to talk to you teens about the way they are dressing, keep in mind that teenagers, like people in general, are more responsive to subtle suggestions than coercion. Instead of asking your teen to change her clothes immediately, try simply suggesting that a skirt just a little bit longer may be better for school. Coercion invariably leads to an angry child; subtle suggestions may not be responded to in the moment but should get the point across over time. Your teenagers will respond best and are more likely to be persuaded when they trust your intentions. Making your teenagers aware of the impact of their clothes on others, for example, will be more effective than "Take that off or you are not leaving this house!" Your daughters may not be aware of their blossoming sexuality and its effect on those around them. Your son may not be aware that his clothing choices project a "bad boy" sort of image. Gentle guidance such as "You look great, but try pulling your shirt down a little," or "You look handsome so please tuck your boxers in a bit," will be better met than "You look terrible."

At all times keep in mind that your teenagers are struggling to get it right; just like you sometimes struggle to get your outfit right for work or for that formal benefit dinner. Consider how you would feel if you were told "You look totally inappropriate," rather than "You look lovely, that blouse would look even better tucked in."

I DON'T KNOW:

1. A sincere expression indicating a lack of knowledge regarding an issue or topic.
PARENT: "Is Jesse going to the party also?"
TEENAGER: "I don't know."
SUGGESTED PARENTAL RESPONSE: A response that honors your teen's sincerity. In the example above you can respond: "Well, I guess you will find out when you get there."

2. An expression of irritability or annoyance regarding a question to which a teen may not want to provide the answer.
PARENT: "How did everyone else do on the test?"
TEENAGER: "I don't know!"
SUGGESTED PARENTAL RESPONSE: Acknowledge that you may have asked the wrong question. You can try again with a statement that shows that you are interested in your teen. For the example above: "I'm sorry. You're right. I am only interested in you."

Tattoos and Piercings

Perhaps of even more concern to parents is that body modification practices—tattoos and piercings—are becoming increasingly common in the adolescent population. Today, many adolescents consider body piercings and tattoos fashionable. However, you should know that many adolescents do not get tattoos and piercings impulsively. Often these are well thought out behaviors. If you are willing to discuss these topics with your teens you can talk to them about health and safety issues and your concern that they exercise caution and good judgment—after all, a tattoo lasts forever. In an upbeat and vivacious teenager there is probably little to be concerned about if they ask about getting a tattoo or piercing. If you really have difficulty getting past your own feelings of resistance try a compromise. Instead of piercings agree to stick on or magnetic body decorations that look like piercings. Henna tattoos (a special natural dye which is not permanent) can be a compromise to permanent tattoos.

GET THEM TALKING

"That outfit looks great, but a different top would make it look even more beautiful."

You can expect your teens to not only be more likely to listen to you but also more likely to discuss their clothing choices without dismissing you. This is because you are being positive, not critical.

If your teenagers begin to request frequent piercings and/or tattoos at a young age and this is a significant change in style then we encourage you to talk more about this with them. It is important to discern if your teens want to get these modifications due to loneliness or because they feel deprived of social attention. If you are concerned that this may be the case, a positive attitude toward a professional evaluation might be warranted.

DOOR SLAMMING:

1. A behavior indicating a need to be alone.

PARENT: "How was school today?"

TEENAGER: Slams door.

SUGGESTED PARENTAL RESPONSE: "If you want to talk later, I'll be here." Leave yourself open for communication at a later time.

2. A message that the teenager is upset and wants you to be aware of that.

PARENT: "Did that test go okay?"

TEENAGER: Slams door.

SUGGESTED PARENTAL RESPONSE: Provide emotional support. "I was worried about that. When you're ready I'd love to hear what happened."

3. A behavior indicating confusion.

PARENT: "Hi."

TEENAGER: Slams door.

SUGGESTED PARENTAL RESPONSE: Your teenager may be feeling confused about things. After all, you didn't request much. You simply said "Hi." Do not attempt to continue the conversation at this time.

I Liked It Better When She Dressed Up Because It Was Halloween!

There are additional teen styles that may worry you. The *Goth* style of black clothing and pale makeup consistently concerns many parents. In our work with adolescents, we have often noted that this style seems to appeal to teens who don't feel that they fit in with their conformist peers (in a sense they are actually conforming to nonconformity). Another teen style that sometimes concerns parents is referred to as *Emo* and is characterized by a tight clothing style, hair that is often colored, straight, and covers the eyes, and a preference for emotional and confessional music. At this point there is no reason to believe that there is a direct connection between clothing style, musical taste, and emotional well-being. Some teens may be attempting to express a form of creativity and self-expression while other teens may feel awkward and self-conscious and be inadvertently expressing gloom and doom. It can be stressful trying to figure out when and if to be concerned, and getting to know your teenagers is the only way to find out what they are really trying to express. The best rule of thumb is as follows: Unless there is a dramatic change in style, there is usually little reason to worry.

Do the Clothes Make the Teen? Helping Your Teens Understand the Messages They May Be Relaying

Some have argued that the influence of today's media has resulted in teens who are far more sophisticated and savvy than previous generations. It may feel as if your kids are growing up more quickly and, in many ways, this may be accurate. It is important for you to realize that just because your kids mimic the grown-up behaviors that they see on television and in movies in the ways that they talk and dress, does not mean that they possess an understanding of how they are presenting themselves. Basically, fast talk and provocative dress do not necessarily mean fast action. This is a time when we recommend that you create opportunities to talk with your teens about how what they are seeing and hearing in the media influences their behaviors.

Girls who mature early need to be especially aware of the effect their clothing choices have on how others react to them. They may dress in a more mature fashion than is age appropriate to display their changing bodies. On the other hand, they may have no idea that their tight-fitting and/or revealing clothing may accentuate their more mature figures. These girls may have to deal with older boys who demonstrate sexual interest in them. We recommend that you engage in honest and open conversation with these early bloomers so that they understand the impact that their clothing choices may have on boys' expectations of them.

Boys who mature early have similar problems. The adults in their lives may assume that their behavior will be consistent with their older looks. As a result, authority figures such as teachers, coaches, and sometimes parents may have greater expectations than they do of their younger-looking peers. You should be particularly aware of how these boys present themselves. For example, do you really want your thirteen-year-old son to grow a mustache or goatee?

Parents Be Aware of What You Wear

On occasion, teenagers we are working with will come in complaining about what their parents are wearing. They dislike it when parents dress like teenagers and would rather they dress in an age-appropriate manner. These teenagers want you to look like adults, not like their peers. Clearly they get embarrassed and may also feel like you are somehow competing with them. It is confusing for your teens when you dress like a teenager, but expect to be sought after for parental adult advice. Teens often identify dress with behavior so if you dress too young you may inadvertently send the message to your teens that you do not/cannot be depended upon the way other parents who dress their age can be. With this in mind we caution against the following (as reported to us by the teens with whom we have worked):

MOTHERS RECONSIDER
- Midriff and tube tops.
- Low necklines.
- Short shorts.
- Thigh-high mini skirts (would your mother approve?).
- Low-rise jeans with a lot of skin showing.
- Skimpy bikinis.
- Sheer clothing.
- Jeans with holes in all the wrong places.

FATHERS RECONSIDER
- Skin-tight jeans.
- Slacks that show the crack of your buttocks.
- Skimpy bathing suits (particularly Speedos).
- Boxers visible above low- or drop-waist baggy pants.
- Boxers sticking out under shorts' legs.
- T-shirts bearing demeaning, vulgar, or drug-related messages.

- Jewelry with illegal drug charms, sexual references such as play-boy bunny charms, or violent references such as guns or knives.
- Jeans with holes in all the wrong places.

We want to clarify, that just because we are advocating that you dress your age, we are not suggesting that you refrain from dressing fashionably. Isn't it ironic, that while you may express worry and concern when your teens dress too grown-up your teens may get upset and embarrassed if you dress too young?

THANKS (THANKS A LOT):

1. A simple expression of appreciation, nothing more.
PARENT: "Yes, I can drive you there."
TEENAGER: "Thanks."
SUGGESTED PARENTAL RESPONSE: A simple acknowledgment of the teen's good manners such as, "You're welcome."

2. When said sarcastically, a simple expression of anger and/or disappointment.
PARENT: "Your father and I have decided not to let you go to the concert."
TEENAGER: "Thanks a lot."
SUGGESTED PARENTAL RESPONSE: "Sorry, when you're ready to talk to me maybe we can come up with some other fun things to do." In all cases, avoid responding sarcastically.

LET'S REVIEW: TIPS FOR TRANSLATING

You have now learned all you need to know about what your teens may not be saying out loud. Just keep the following points in mind and you are well on your way to understanding how to interpret the many nuances involved when talking *Teenage*.

1. **It's Not Always What They Say but How They Say It:** By understanding how to interpret your teen's body language your comprehension of *Teenage* will be greatly enhanced.

2. **Sometimes Actions Speak Louder Than Words:** Your teens may relate some level of distress through changes in behavior. Your keen eyes and a little bit of understanding will go a long way once you know what to look for.

3. **Communicate Concern and Caring Without Using Words:** Be mindful of the nonverbal messages you send your teens. By using body language you can encourage your teen to engage with you.

4. **Subtlety Always Trumps Coercion:** Your teens will listen to subtle suggestions about their clothing choices. Demands that they change clothes immediately will lead to rage and acting out and it may damage the quality of the relationship.

5. **Dress Your Role, Your Teen Is Watching:** Parents who dress like teens, but want to be viewed as adults confuse teens. By making appropriate clothing choices and engaging in good grooming practices, you are teaching your teen that taking care of the outside contributes to feeling good on the inside.

CHAPTER 4

Requests for Independence: When "Back Off" Really Means "Back Me Up"

Remember when your teens were around two or three? Back then "No" and "I can do it" were probably among their favorite words. That was a time when your children began affirming their independence and they wanted to do and try everything on their own. It was as if their eyes suddenly opened and they discovered the wonderful world around them. Although they were excited to explore the world on their own, it was also important for them to know that you were nearby watching. On occasion this big new world would become overwhelming and they would run into your arms when a bit frightened or scared. Other times their attempt to "do it" resulted in failure and they would feel overcome by frustration. You may still treasure the memories of those moments when they ran back to you for a comforting hug or kiss.

Now fast forward to the present. Your teen tells you about the expensive new gadget he is planning to buy with his job money. You may not say this out loud, but you are perplexed. After all, didn't he tell you he was getting the job so he could save money for college? You contemplate pointing this out. His recent responses to similar questions, however, have been met with annoyed reassurances that he knows what he is doing. You are left feeling unsure of how or if to respond.

Before you start to worry, realize that adolescence is a time of awakening for most teens. As their ability for abstract thinking has developed (as discussed in Chapter 1) so has their acknowledgment of the world at large. This results in an excitement about the outside world and a newfound determination to do and try things on their own. This is a time when you once again find yourself in the role of active observer. While your adolescents assert their independence by stepping up, the role for you is to learn to strike a balance between stepping in and stepping aside.

Negotiating the See Saw

Adolescents don't generally wake up one day and announce to their parents that they want to be independent. Instead, the process tends to be a gradual one. When you and your teens work together, the road to independence is a lot less bumpy. You should be aware, though, that the road is not without its potholes—your role is to provide the right balance of support and structure to help your teen negotiate around them.

In order to strike the balance it is important to understand how to manage the process. If you encourage your teens' independence at too early an age, they may experience difficulties in later adolescence. This is because they are left feeling that they are expected do things on their own, without your support. As your teens get older the situations they are left to manage become more complex. If your teens do not feel as if they can turn to you, they are left feeling overwhelmed and incompetent. They may mismanage situations because they fail to seek support and advice from the more experienced, competent adults around them.

The goal of achieving independence is accomplished by encouraging your teens to do and try new things. It is important, however, to provide some structure and guidance. You wouldn't tell a teen who has never been behind the wheel, "Here are the keys to the car, you learn best by doing." On the other hand, if your teens are anxious about learning to drive you shouldn't discourage them from learning. The best way for your teens to become competent in the world is to go out and face its challenges. Just as you persuaded your child to join the birthday party when he clung to you at age two or three, teens are most successful when they are encouraged to be self-reliant and independent, to stand on their own.

Independence and Autonomy

Before we move on to discuss the specifics of becoming independent, it is important to explain the difference between independence and autonomy—after all, this is a book about language. In *Teenage* the difference translates like this: You promote autonomy by encouraging your teens to negotiate the world at large. This entails providing structure, support, and guidelines on how to proceed on an as-needed basis. You promote independence when you encourage your teens to negotiate the world on their own. This means your teens are supported in trying new things and managing situations on their own. Autonomy eventually leads to independence. As already suggested, there is a balance that needs to be established between encouraging independence and autonomy. It is important to provide the right type of structure and support. If your teens experience you as too controlling, blaming, or even rejecting, they are at higher risk for difficulties including alcohol and substance abuse, eating disorders, and self-injurious behaviors. Your teens may see themselves as more autonomous and independent than you see them. This perception may be due to your encouraging your teens' to be more autonomous and independent when you perceive them to be acting more self-reliant. In turn, your teens act more self-reliant because of this encouragement.

In the quest for independence it is quite common for you and your teens to experience conflict; you may notice that your teens seem increasingly emotionally and even physically distant. Some have gone as far as to suggest that tension and disagreement are not only to be expected but are necessary for your teens to become mature, free-thinking, self-reliant individuals. We always caution that there are exceptions to the general rules. If you and your teens continue to maintain a close personal and emotional relationship with little conflict you should not be concerned. Your job is to encourage independence and self-reliance. Their job is to demonstrate their abilities to make responsible independent decisions and judgments about themselves and the world around them.

"But, Johnny's parents let him . . . ." Is Timing Everything?

On the road to independence there are many issues and concerns that arise. The hot topics are many and you are often faced with a barrage of questions and requests. The pressure from your teens can be, at times, overwhelming. In both pre-adolescence (or tweenhood) and early adolescence conflicts often focus on technology use. You, for example, contemplate when or if to buy them a cell phone. In older adolescence, dating, driving, and applying to college appear to be among the most stressful topics to negotiate. Many of the conflicts are age-dependent. "How young is too young?" you may wonder. Unfortunately, there is no easy answer to this question. Each child matures at a different rate and, as a parent, it is important to take the individual into account. There is comforting news, however. If you focus on how you encourage independence in your child instead of when, you can ensure a successful experience.

You may look to other parents to help you decide when you should allow your teens to do certain things. And, in fact, your teens may pressure you by pointing out what their friends are already being permitted to do by their parents. Invariably, according to your teen, there is always one kid who is permitted to do it all. The pressure from your children can, at times, become difficult to resist. Their enthusiasm about something may suggest that they are ready. The question you then need to ask yourself is, "How ready am I?" Keep in mind our mantra, "When your parents aren't anxious, life is beautiful." If you let your children do something that you are not comfortable with, your own anxiety can impact their experiences. When people are anxious they often become controlling and irritable. You do not want to send your teen off to assert their independence while responding in this manner. The best approach is to offer support and guidance. This sends the message that you are encouraging your teens' independence, but are available to help them negotiate the newfound challenges that they may face.

Interestingly, it has been noted that less independent teens experience lower levels of stress in adolescence but have greater difficulty facing the world on their own once they reach adulthood. This may be because they are so comfortable in their lives and so strongly attached to their parents that they are sheltered from the outside world. Parents of these teens may contribute to this by not encouraging—or, in some cases, actually discouraging—them to be independent. These teens have not been given the opportunities to build up the skills necessary to live independent lives. When your teens feel they are encouraged and supported by you, they tend to work harder, achieve more, and report feeling satisfaction in a job well done. Your teens will possess the skills necessary to negotiate the outside world in large part because you have encouraged their independence while continuing to offer the structure, support, and guidance when needed.

Changes in Peer Group—It Was Easier When You Made the Play Dates

Developmentally speaking, an important shift occurs when your teenagers begin to rely less on your support and opinions and more on those of their friends. As your children grow into teens your role in their peer relationships makes a shift. This change entails you moving from direct involvement in their peer relationships (i.e., establishing and maintaining their friendships by setting up play dates or sending out invitations to birthday parties, etc.) to monitoring their peer relationships (e.g., permitting them to go places, insisting that they call while out, etc.). As we discussed in Chapter 2, some degree of monitoring is effective. It has been found that even teens monitored after school only via phone are less likely to give in to negative peer pressure than teens who are not monitored at all.

But how do your teens choose their friends? Well, teens typically choose peers who they perceive as possessing similar values and interests. This, however, can pose a dilemma. Because your teens tend to pick friends with whom they closely identify they may encourage and support each other to engage in both negative and positive behaviors. Luckily, peer influence is only one of many factors that can contribute to your teen engaging in high-risk behaviors. The bottom line is this: It is important to know with whom your teens are spending time. Where and when they have met each particular friend can be telling as well. How and when you ask the questions can greatly affect the likelihood of a response.

At times it is difficult not to judge a book by its cover; if you have concerns about your teens' friends because of the way they look, take the opportunity to get to know them first. It is important to evaluate each of your teens' friends within context. If, for example, your daughter has one friend who has an offbeat style of dress and makeup, it is a different situation than if you suddenly notice that all of her friends look this way. Also, it is important to note whether or not your daughter has changed her appearance (as we discussed in Chapter 3). Putting your concerns on the table in an honest yet gentle manner is not only important, but it may be invaluable. Many parents make the mistake of avoidance. Instead of directly talking to their teens about concerns related to their peer group, they try to control the situation by changing the rules depending on the friend involved. Such inconsistency always backfires. Quite frankly, it encourages your teens to "work the system." Your daughter, for example, says she is with Amy when she is really with Liz. You are bound to find out eventually and you know that can lead to nothing but disagreement and conflict. Encourage your teens to be open and honest with you; it is important that you model good behavior by offering them the same! Work with your teens to create a plan that addresses any concerns you may have about their whereabouts including with whom they are spending time.

I HATE YOU:

1. An expression used to strongly convey anger in the moment.
PARENT: "No." (In response to an unreasonable request.)
TEENAGER: "I hate you!"
SUGGESTED PARENTAL RESPONSE: "I'm sorry that you're upset, but that isn't going to change my answer."

2. A high impact expression used primarily for "shock value" in an attempt to secure some "alone time."
PARENT: "Your sister didn't think that that teacher was such a hard grader." (Verbalized with no malicious intent.)
TEENAGER: "I hate you! You always compare me to her!"
SUGGESTED PARENTAL RESPONSE: "I didn't mean to upset you. Maybe we can talk more later after you take some cooling down time."

3. A verbalization used as a last ditch effort to get a parent to change his/her mind.
PARENT: "No." (In response to an unreasonable request.)
TEENAGER: "All of my friends are going! I hate you!"
SUGGESTED PARENTAL RESPONSE: None. Wait until later to discuss or revisit the issue.

In order to avoid conflict, set the rules regarding new friends in advance. Once again, collaborate with your teenagers to create a policy that makes everyone comfortable. Encourage your teens to invite new friends over to your home so that you have an opportunity to get to know them. If your teens want to go over to unknown friends' homes, insist on direct contact with the new friends' parents. In a nonconfrontational way, encourage your teens to tell you about their new friends. For example: "It sounds like you and Liz are becoming good friends. What do you like about her? What does she like to do for fun? Is she in any of your classes?" Also take the opportunity to get to know new friends when they are in your home (more about this in Chapter 5). Ask them about their interests and other light topics. If you are already in a situation where you have lost some trust in your teens due to previous incidents, create a plan that allows them to rebuild the trust. We often recommend parents implement the Random Stop-by Rule outlined in Chapter 2.

GET THEM TALKING

"She seems like a fun friend."

Praise rather than criticism is more likely to open up a dialogue about friends.

Trust your instincts if you are concerned that your teens are suddenly involved with a negative peer group, not involved with a peer group, or have distanced themselves from their peers. These may be signs that a professional evaluation is warranted.

Remember When a Date Wasn't Just a Day on a Calendar?

If you are the parent of a teen involved in a significant relationship you may be scratching your head wondering how your son and his girlfriend got together. You don't remember any mention of dates. All you know is that one day your son showed up with this girl acting as if you knew that they were together. Today, the meaning of the term dating has shifted slightly. It is now rarely used to describe a discrete situation and is more often used to describe a relationship status.

You may be relieved to know, however, that while the process of dating has changed somewhat, the rules and expectations have generally remained the same.

Who Is This Guy Romeo and Why Does My Daughter Keep Insisting They Are "Just Friends"?

There is no magic age at which kids demonstrate an interest in the opposite sex. It is not uncommon to hear tweens (especially girls) talking and laughing about the opposite sex in their middle-school classes. This flirty banter may signify the beginning of interest. While at younger ages your kids' ability to spend time together outside of school is mediated by you, it is generally during the tween years (roughly between ages eight and twelve) that boys and girls start socializing together. In fact, today girls and boys interact much more frequently than in the past. This can make it difficult for you to figure out if acquaintances of the opposite sex are merely friends or something more.

It is often in middle school that kids begin going out together in large coed groups. Coed parties are quite common and may also provide opportunities for couples to spend time together. A relatively new phenomenon is coed sleepovers. If you are willing to host a coed party and/or sleepover we recommend that you work out the details with your children in advance. You need to consider the level of supervision you will provide. Do you intend to be present in the room the entire night, or simply be randomly checking in? If this is a sleepover, will boys and girls be sleeping in the same room? If so, will you divide the room up, boys on one side, girls on the other, or will you allow the kids to sleep wherever? A good way to determine the issues you need to address is to put yourself in the shoes of a parent of a child you may not know that well. What questions and answers would put you at ease? In addition, if you are planning a coed sleepover do not assume that each child will notify their parents of this fact. We are pretty sure that, given the opportunity, some kids will leave out this fact when telling their parents about the party in an effort to avoid conflict with their parents. Therefore, it is important to acknowledge the coed nature of the party on the invitation. This will provide parents with the opportunity to make their own decisions.

Sexting

Technology has also had an impact on the coed socialization process. Texting and social networking provide a way for tweens and teens to communicate regularly in a somewhat indirect way. We have heard of many tween and teen relationships that begin via texting and Facebook wall writing. However, as discussed in Chapter 2, this technology also allows tweens and teens to assert themselves more independently without your involvement.

Sexting, sending sexually explicit texts, photos, or even videos via cell phone, has gained popularity among some teens. Boys are more likely to engage in verbal sexting—writing explicit messages to girls that they may like. Girls, on the other hand, tend to engage in all three sexting behaviors; when a girl likes a boy she may send him explicit pictures or videos of herself to him. As with many adolescent behaviors this is often peer influenced. Teens who have friends who find this behavior acceptable are more likely to engage in it themselves.

With regard to dating, teens sometimes use sexting as a flirting mechanism, but it is also used by teens who are already romantically involved, much the way couples use phone sex. In this scenario, couples interact by texting explicit material back and forth. However, the difference between phone sex and sexting is clear. Phone conversations do not generally end up leaving permanent records on the Internet or able to be sent to large groups of people. But teens who engage in sexting run the risk of unintentionally being exposed to both their friends and strangers. It is important for you to explain the risks of sexting to your children. The broadcasting of these private texts often devastates teens who feel embarrassed, ashamed, and betrayed. In addition to the risk to your children's reputations, such activity may put them at risk with the law.

You can imagine the shock of parents who have either read their kids' explicit texts or seen the pictures or videos sent. We must caution you that it is difficult to know if your teens engage in this behavior. We have been privy to the most explicit texts sent by kids with whom we have worked. We can assure you that the content took us by surprise and reaffirmed that you cannot judge children by how they present themselves. The seemingly sweetest and most respectful kids can also be the authors of the most vulgar and explicit texts. As always, the best approach with your teens is to be proactive (follow the guidelines presented in Chapter 2).

Dating

During early dating (in early adolescence) your teens generally expect your involvement although they may act as if they don't. We suggest that you respond by managing your young teens' dating experiences the same way you manage their other peer relationships: by being a consultant to them. During these early years it is important for you to discuss rules and limits. If you promote your teens' autonomy in dating experiences (e.g., offer support and guidance without controlling) your teens are more likely to report positive romantic experiences, and your advice and guidance in these early years will not only be accepted, but sought after.

GET THEM TALKING

"Would you recommend the movie you saw last night?"
This indirect request for information about how the date went may encourage your teens to comment on the movie and then segue into a conversation about the date.

A great way to impart a good relationship to your teens is to model one yourself. Exposure to high levels of conflict between you and your partner, for example, can put your teens at greater risk for experiencing conflict in their own romantic relationships. In addition if your home has been characterized by marital instability including separation, divorce, and/or remarriage your teens are more likely to be involved in romantic relationships at a younger age. If your young teens cannot find emotional stability in your home, then they may attempt to create the stability through their own relationships. Since kids in their early teens often lack the insight and emotional maturity of older teens, these early romantic relationships can put them at greater risk for relationships characterized by conflict or abuse. In general, your teens may then be involved in romantic relationships characterized by greater intensity and dependence than other teens.

Is She Really Going Out with Him?

Take a moment to think back to your own teenage years. Remember your first love interest or crush? What did your parents think of him or her? Romantic relationships are sometimes a source of stress for your teens. You can contribute to this stress when you are quick to judge or react negatively to your teens' romantic choices. Meeting your son or daughters' significant others can be stressful for everyone. Your teens probably do not realize that you may feel as stressed in these situations as they do. It is helpful if you create situations that are comfortable and casual. Giving your daughter's boyfriend the third degree may be effective in the movies, but in reality the only thing that it can accomplish is embarrassment.

I've Tried, but I'm Just Not That Into Her

Your sixteen-year-old son announces that he has met the love of his life! You too have met the lucky girl on a number of occasions.

Although you may contend that you have tried to see what he sees, you just don't and you can't imagine that you ever will. What should you do? As long as their dating does not pose any real threat to your son's safety or well-being, our advice is to do nothing! After all, you're not the one dating her!

If you're having trouble interacting with your teen's significant other, the following table offers some helpful suggestions.

TRY THIS	RATHER THAN THIS
Resist the urge to judge or react negatively when you meet your teen's significant other for the first time.	Widen your eyes and stare down the young man in front of you. Ask him if his parents actually let him out of the house dressed the way he is.
Engage your teen's romantic partner in casual conversation. Invite him to sit down. Talk in a calm and gentle tone in an effort to put him at ease. Avoid direct and confrontational questions.	Give your teen's date the third degree. Make it clear that if he hurts your teen or tries to take advantage in any way he will have to deal with you. Embarrass him by asking direct intrusive questions such as "Are you planning to have sex with my daughter?"
Create opportunities to get to know your teen's romantic partner especially if you have a negative first impression. Invite him to dinner or family events. This will provide opportunities for you to get to know him better.	Encourage your teen to stop seeing him. You've met him once and that's enough for both of you. Create opportunities to speak negatively about him. Hope that eventually your daughter will see that you are right and dump him.

Remember, this is a time to be thoughtful. If your teens have had a series of romantic interests, think back. Have you liked any of them? If the answer is "no" you may need to think about what this is bringing up for you. When your teens start dating it is one more reminder to you that your children are growing up. Ask yourself if your dislike is genuine or whether it actually stems from your own instinct to protect your teens from the emotional pain that can sometimes result from the end of a romantic relationship. Perhaps your opinions stem from your wish to avoid the fact that not too long ago, your children only had eyes for you. Will anyone ever be good enough? If these explanations don't seem to apply, consider this: These early relationships help your teens grow and learn. These encounters can impact future experience in adolescence and adulthood. The more experience your teens gain in negotiating romantic relationships, the better equipped they will be to manage relationships in adulthood. The relationships your teens have with you can also contribute to this development. Adolescents who feel unsupported or who are not strongly emotionally connected to their parents are more likely to seek out that support in romantic partners. If your teens have positive relationships with you they are more likely to engage in romantic relationships marked by acceptance, satisfaction, and love.

Your teens' romantic relationships will increase in importance as they get older and rules should be developed accordingly. Rules created to supervise dating activities reflect a healthy parent–child relationship, but rules created to prescribe or dictate the type of person your teens should be dating and what they should be doing are less effective. For example, if you are less than pleased with your daughter's boyfriend, creating a rule which limits her from seeing him is not necessarily recommended. You may be patting yourself on the back because you believe that your mission to rid your daughter of her unacceptable romantic partner has been accomplished. However, your confidence may decrease when you learn that, in reality, she may have stopped bringing him around because she does not want to subject him to your criticism. Your concerns about your teens' significant others are best addressed by creating a set of fair rules that apply regardless of whether or not you are pleased with a particular partner. This will be perceived as less judgmental. Your teens are better served when you collaborate with them to develop rules, which provide greater opportunities for you to supervise their activities fairly.

Sometimes Rumors Are True—What to Do If the News about Her Boyfriend Is Not Good

On occasion, you may receive discouraging information from outside sources regarding the character of your teens' significant others. Before jumping to conclusions, we encourage you to consider the source. If the information seems relatively reliable it is important for you to approach your teen in a calm and nonconfrontational manner. It is highly likely that your teens are already aware of the rumors. While you must then decide what actions to take—if any—it is important that your teens are given opportunities to address the issues in calm, supportive, and interactive discussions. Provide opportunities to listen and to hear what your teens have to say. In some cases, you may decide that the only course of action available is to prohibit your teen from dating a particular individual. This may be the case if you believe allowing your child to continue the relationship would pose safety risks. While such a discussion is not likely to be easy, the more caring and concerned you are when you bring up the matter, the more your teen is likely to feel understood and supported. If your concerns relate to safety and a compromise is not possible, clearly highlight the concerns and consequences if your teen refuses to end the relationship and discuss the ways you intend to monitor the situation.

ARMS CROSSED TIGHTLY:

1. A gesture conveying anger.
PARENT: "I really dislike your boyfriend."

TEENAGER: Crosses arms tightly.

SUGGESTED PARENTAL RESPONSE: Try this again in a less direct and a more gentle manner. Remember teens are more responsive to indirect requests for information. Try "I'd like to get to know your boyfriend better."

2. A gesture conveying defensiveness or a need to protect against perceived criticism.
PARENT: "Don't you think your jeans are too tight?"

TEENAGER: Crosses arms tightly.

SUGGESTED PARENTAL RESPONSE: Try again. "You look nice; are your jeans comfortable?"

3. An attempt to soothe or comfort self.
PARENT: "That must have been disappointing."

TEENAGER: Crosses arms tightly.

SUGGESTED PARENTAL RESPONSE: None. Perhaps your teen simply doesn't want to talk at this moment.

Your teens probably respect your opinions regarding dating issues although they are likely to keep that fact private. Surprisingly, most teens consider their parents better sources for information about romance than their friends or romantic partners. Teens who express that their parents offer a balance of guidance and support, also report having more positive romantic relationships than other teens. They are also more likely to discuss their romantic relationships with their parents and to seek advice when needed. As always, you need to maintain a balance when involving yourself in the romantic affairs of your teens.

GET THEM TALKING

"Your boyfriend has a good sense of humor."
Start positively and get them talking about someone that you are interested in finding out more about.

Your teens are more likely to disclose information regarding their romantic relationships with you when the process is interactive. In turn, when your teens self-disclose you are more likely to get information than if you make attempts to actively monitor their dating activities. When you work with your teens to create a set of dating guidelines and rules, you model confidence and caring to them. While there is no guarantee that these practices will result in positive romantic relationships, this approach does offer your teens the support and guidance they may need as they navigate through these early romantic interludes.

As your teens get older, driving may become part of the dating conversation. This can be an equally sensitive area an equally sensitive area that needs to be communicated about is driving and everything it entails. Like dating, it can be a very emotional topic.

The Business of Learning to Drive

It is extremely important to communicate clearly and sensitively with your teen when teaching him to drive. Safe habits are established at this point and, as we know, teens like to talk when they are in the car. So take a drive with your teen! This is a perfect opportunity for you to talk with him about driving.

Ask any teen who is currently learning to drive to name the adult they prefer to drive with and they can tell you without skipping a beat. Think back to your own early driving experiences and we bet you can quickly report with whom you were most comfortable. Learning to drive can be a stressful experience for both you and your teens and some parents are better equipped than others to teach their teens how to drive. If possible, acknowledge the best candidate for the job before you and your teen get in the car and talk to your teen to make sure that she agrees. If you're having trouble talking to your teen about driving—or staying calm when on the road—see the following chart for some ideas:

TRY THIS	RATHER THAN THIS
Ask your teens with whom they think they would be most comfortable learning to drive.	Tell your teens who is going to teach them to drive. If they seem concerned about the choice tell them "Tough luck."
Choose the calmest and least emotionally reactive adult to be your teen's driving teacher.	Choose the person who is the most anxious and emotionally reactive.
While driving with your teens, offer directives and feedback in a calm and controlled tone of voice.	Yell directives and obscenities at your teens when they do something incorrect or concerning.
Ask your teen to pull over and park the car and then calmly talk with them about any concerns or suggestions.	Stomp the ground as if you are braking, grab onto the side of the car as if holding on for dear life, or push them aside, and take the wheel while they are driving.

TRY THIS	RATHER THAN THIS
After each lesson quickly review both their strengths and weaknesses. Offer them constructive criticism if necessary.	After the lesson tell them they are dangerous and shouldn't be on the road because you are afraid they will kill either themselves or someone else.
If it is clear that they need more off-road practice suggest a wide-open, empty lot to which you can take them to continue with their lessons. Encourage them to keep practicing with you because driving is a skill that takes time to learn.	Discourage them from learning to drive. Tell them they are better off taking the bus or even walking.

Keys to the Car Should Be Synonymous with Both Caring and Cooperation

To teens, few opportunities represent the true spirit of independence more than the ability to drive. When you allow your teens to drive you offer up far more than a set of keys. In addition to the obvious responsibilities related to driving (i.e., following the speed limit, heeding traffic signs and lights, etc.) there are other responsibilities that are exchanged for the car keys. Quite commonly, driving teens are assigned the carpooling duties for younger siblings in exchange for their own independent use of the car or asked to run errands such as grocery shopping or picking up the dry cleaning. In our experience, most teens are agreeable to these responsibilities. On occasion, however, these responsibilities can become so overwhelming that they begin to impinge on a teen's ability to fulfill the rest of his responsibilities, such as completing schoolwork, in a timely manner. Meanwhile, you may be so relieved that some of your own burdens are lifted by your teenager's ability to drive that you may forget to check in with him about how he feels. You may assume that because he can drive, these are tasks he will want to do. In fact, we have met more than a few teens who are so overwhelmed by their own driving-related anxiety that they actually begin to hate driving. As with most topics, it is important for you to sit down and talk with your teens about their feelings about driving. In addition, a structured conversation should focus on establishing a set of guidelines including rules and consequences related to driving activities. You need to reaffirm to your teens who may be overzealous about driving that it is a privilege, not necessarily a right. By pre-establishing an understanding before handing over the keys, conflicts can be avoided. We sometimes hear from parents who express concerns related to their teens' involvement in irresponsible, high-risk behaviors such as drug abuse, excessive drinking, vandalism, and stealing to name a few. Nonetheless, these parents have willingly handed over the car keys to their teens. We are surprised when these parents report that they did not realize they were *allowed* to take the car keys away as a consequence to unrelated yet concerning inappropriate behaviors. Although your teens may protest rules (as discussed in Chapter 1), in general, rules are expected and your teens will respect you for putting them into place. When you emphasize the great responsibility related to driving you send a message of importance to your teens and if they can't handle the responsibility you must react and respond appropriately. Before they even begin driving, work with your teens to create a structured list of driving rules, including the associated consequences for breaking each rule.

Make an Impact

While driving is by nature an independent activity, you can make an impact on your teens' driving behaviors. It has been demonstrated that if you are aware of where your teens are and what they are doing they are less likely to engage in risky driving behaviors and, as a result, are at lower risk to be involved in an accident. In addition, they may be at lower risk for traffic violations. By taking an active role in developing rules related to driving you can actually help ensure that your teens drive responsibly. Although it may be difficult to know how safe your teens are when you are not in the car with them, there are ways to predict whether they are more prone to risky driving behaviors. By taking on the role of active participant, you may be able to garner information about the type of drivers your teens will be even before they ever get behind the wheel.

GET THEM TALKING

"It must be hard to say no to them when they ask you for rides."
Your teens are more likely to discuss peer pressure if you introduce the topic subtly and without judgment.

Watch, listen, and learn about the driving habits of their friends. Ask your teens about their friends' driving in a calm, casual manner. If your teens report that their friends engage in risky driving behaviors such as speeding and/or weaving in and out of lanes these may be red flags, especially if your teens have been in the car with these friends. Ask your teens if their friends have gotten any tickets for driving. When your teens drive in cars with friends who engage in high-risk driving behaviors these behaviors become more familiar and there-fore more acceptable. Every time your teens do not get in an accident when they or a friend is driving and engaging in risky driving behavior, it increases the likelihood that they perceive these behaviors as acceptable and not dangerous.

In addition to being influenced by the driving behaviors of their friends, your teens also look to you. Be sure to model appropriate driving behavior to your teens. If you are a particularly aggressive driver your teens are more likely to consider these behaviors acceptable. Avoid talking on your cell phone or yelling at other cars if they are in your way and, especially, don't drink and drive—even if you've only had a few. If you model these behaviors, don't expect your teens not to engage in them just because you tell them not to.

Drinking and Driving

The good news is that, compared to adults, teens are less likely to drive after drinking. Unfortunately, when teens do drink and drive the risk of them being involved in a crash is greatly increased in comparison to adults. We are not suggesting that either adults or teens engage in such behavior. It is important, however, for you to educate your teens about the perils of drinking and driving. The combination of talking to your teens about safety and modeling safe driving practices yourself is sure to make a positive impact. If your teens are overwhelmed by stress and have a history of drinking as a way to cope with stress they are at higher risk of engaging in drinking and driving. It will probably come as no surprise that your teens are at greater risk to drink and drive if you do not enforce any restrictions on driving and are unaware of their driving practices.

Here are some guidelines to help you bring up the topic of drinking and driving with your teens:

TRY THIS	RATHER THAN THIS
"Did you see the article about the kids who got killed driving drunk? That is so sad."	"Did you read about those stupid teenagers who got killed because they were drinking and driving?"
"I don't want you to be in any dangerous situations so let's talk about how you'll handle things if you need a ride and the driver has been drinking. Let's make a 911 plan."	"If I hear that you even thought about getting into a car with a friend who has been drinking there will be consequences!"
"Did I ever tell you about my high school friend who got into an accident after a party? I still get upset thinking about it."	"I don't know what's wrong with your generation. Do you all have a death wish?"
"I don't want you to drink. What concerns me even more is the thought of you getting hurt in an accident. Let's talk."	"If you or your friends decide to drink and drive, I don't want to know anything about it!"

Driving While on a Cell Phone or Driving While Texting

In recent years, driving while talking or texting on cell phones has become an issue of great concern. Drivers between the ages of sixteen and twenty-four appear to make up the largest percentage of drivers who engage in these activities. In general any distracting behavior (e.g., eating, talking, changing a CD, putting on makeup, reading texts or directions, etc.) increases the risk of an accident. When addressing these concerns with your teens we suggest that you appeal to their common sense. Although we live in a world where multitasking is common, you need to both reinforce and model to your teens that their focus should remain on the road at all times. Remember, as we continue to point out, that so much of what you teach your children is learned through observation.

I DON'T THINK SO:

1. An expression used to convey that you just don't get it.
PARENT: "That is the group of kids that you should be friends with."
TEENAGER: "I don't think so."
SUGGESTED PARENTAL RESPONSE: This may be an opportunity to learn about your teen's feelings. Ask him if he wants to explain his reasons. If not, let it go for now.

2. A gentle response to a harmless question.
PARENT: "Do you want me to suggest you as a babysitter for my colleague at work?"
TEENAGER: "I don't think so."
SUGGESTED PARENTAL RESPONSE: The exchange is finished. You asked a simple question and got an honest answer. Pursue the issue no further. Good work!

Motorcycles

Perhaps you have allowed your teens to have a motorcycle. If your teens prefer hopping on a Harley to driving the family car then encourage them to be responsible and reasonable. Talk to them about how helmets save lives. A substantial portion of motorcycle accidents result in fatalities because the riders (drivers and passengers) are not wearing helmets. Even if you live in a state where helmets are not required by law, this is one rule that is essential for you to enforce. If your teens have inherited this passion from you or your partner, you have a responsibility to model appropriate behavior by following safety guidelines yourself.

Applying to College

The number of high school seniors applying to college has steadily increased over the last several decades. College enrollment is expected to continue to increase at least until 2017. This has inevitably led to increased competition to get into schools. High school seniors have responded to this by applying to more schools than ever before. According to the National Association for Admission Counseling, the percentage of students admitted to each college has decreased slightly in response to both the increase in applications and the decrease of students declining admission to schools. A combination of factors has resulted in the increased number of application submissions including increases in the number of high school graduates, and the ease of applying online. In addition, many students are now using the Common Application, which allows applicants to submit one general application to multiple institutions and avoid filling out separate applications for each.

The college application process results in an intense first semester during senior year for many students. While in the past seniors were able to complete applications in a more leisurely manner, the new deadlines require students to submit the majority of these applications earlier. Pressure from guidance and admission counselors contributes to the stress; and many suggest that in these competitive times, the earlier college applications are submitted, the better.

We realize that the types of applications colleges require can be extremely confusing. Because we know that you can't help or talk to your teens unless you know what they're dealing with, the following list can serve as a quick reference guide for key application terms:

- **Common Application:** A universal application used by many colleges. This allows students to send the same application to many schools. Note that even schools that use the Common Application sometimes require students to complete additional supplementary application sections.
- **Deferred (regarding admission status):** A student is neither admitted to nor rejected from a school to which they applied. Unlike being rejected, a deferred student is still being considered for admission. Sending additional grades, test scores, and recommendations is highly recommended.
- **Deferred (regarding acceptance status):** An accepted student requests a delay in attending the college to which they have been accepted. The majority of schools will allow a student to defer for a year as long as the student provides a reasonable reason and plan for their gap year (see definition below).
- **Early Action:** Students can apply early (most deadlines are before December 1) and find out the colleges' decisions early. If admitted, students are not committed to attend.

- **Early Admission:** When gifted high school juniors are admitted to college early and allowed to skip their senior year. Note that not all schools offer this type of admission. Criteria are very rigorous.

- **Early Admission:** When a student who has not completed high school opts to finish high school requirements in a dual program offered by a community college. An entrance exam is usually required. Students take both high school and college classes simultaneously. Note that not all community colleges offer this option.

- **Early Admission:** An umbrella term used to describe both early action and early decision.

- **Early Decision:** Students can apply early (most deadlines are before December 1) to their top-choice school. If admitted, students are committed to attend.

- **Gap Year:** When an individual decides to take a year off before continuing on with his college education. This term can be used to describe taking off (deferring) a year between graduation from high school and the start of college or taking a year off between one year of college and the next. After graduating college, the term is used to describe taking a year off before pursuing further education or career goals.

- **Rolling Admission:** When a college evaluates and decides about applications for admission as they are received. In general, the earlier applicants apply, the better chance they have of being admitted.

- **Waitlisted:** When a college has completed the review of a student's application and puts them on a waitlist. Whether or not a student is accepted from the waitlist is based on the number of accepted students who commit to attend. It is important to review individual schools' statistics related to admission from waitlist in prior years, as some schools take few if any applicants from the waitlist.

It is helpful to gain a cursory knowledge about the application process prior to talking to your teens. However, you should offer your teens' this information only when engaged in interactive discussions. If you barrage your teens with unsolicited information you may encourage them to shut down and shut out the important information that you are trying to convey. If your teens seem overwhelmed, end the discussion. Find other opportunities to get the information to them. If you have books or pamphlets you think would be helpful either give them to your teens directly or leave them in common areas to which they have easy access, for example, the kitchen or the family room. This way they can read them on their own time.

Whose Application Is It Anyway?

Application time tends to be very stressful for parents as well and you may experience mixed emotions. While you are proud your teens are moving forward in life, you may also feel sad that your teens are growing up. If they are planning to go away to college you may begin to reflect on the fact that they will be home much less frequently. You may take this time to review your own life and figure out what you're going to do once your teens head off to college.

It may also be difficult for you to sit back and watch your teens manage the stress, but the application process itself can serve as a true test of your teens' ability to affirm their independence. For example, you may become frustrated if your teens seem to be procrastinating. We have known more than a few parents who became so overwhelmed, that they could no longer tolerate the stress. In an effort to move the application process along, they have confided to us that they actually completed the applications for their teens. On other occasions we have even heard of parents writing their teens' college essays. We do not recommend this to you. It seems counterintuitive to the process of trying to encourage independence and autonomy in your teens. After all, where do you draw the line? Will you write their term papers once they are enrolled in college? Will you take their midterms or finals? Once your teens graduate and join the work force, do you intend to do their jobs as well? We are clearly taking this to the extreme. Like most parents, you probably acknowledge that these responsibilities belong to your teens. While it may be frustrating that your teens are not operating on the schedule that you might propose, it is important to step back a moment and assess the situation. There are many reasons why your teens may not be accomplishing their tasks in a timely manner. The best way to find out is to sit down with them and ask what is going on. Please do not assume. Ask your teens if they need help. Several common task-related concerns crop up when your teens are applying to college and you may be able to encourage their autonomy by providing the appropriate structure and support. Some common concerns your teens may report that they must contend with include, but certainly aren't limited to, the following:

- Feeling overwhelmed by the task of organizing all the requirements needed to apply to each school (e.g., transcripts, letters of recommendation, etc.).
- Having difficulty writing essays for applications.
- Managing all the competing demands on them resulting from school and outside activities.
- Deciding how many colleges to apply to.
- Developing a list of the colleges to which they should apply.

We provide ideas to help address these concerns in the following table:

TRY THIS	RATHER THAN THIS
If your teens are overwhelmed by the task of organizing information for applications, suggest that they create a spreadsheet that includes the name of each school, the application deadline, and check-off columns for each document that they are required to complete.	Create a spreadsheet yourself and organize the information for them. After all, you are a pro on Excel!
If your teens report they are having difficulty writing their college essays, advise them to just start writing. The best way to generate ideas is to put pen to paper (or fingers to the keyboard). Offer to edit.	Offer to write the essays for them. It's easier than taking the time to sit down and help them edit what they have written.
If your teens report they don't have time to fill out applications due to competing demands, suggest that they put themselves on a schedule. Offer to do what you can to make the time productive (e.g., keep the noise down, refrain from interrupting, etc.).	Offer to complete the applications for them. This will ensure that they will get into a good school.

TRY THIS	RATHER THAN THIS
If your teens are having difficulty deciding how many schools to apply to, suggest they check with outside sources including their school guidance counselors, and friends. Remind them that they will need to include a range of schools from safe (schools to which they are sure they will be accepted) to reach (schools to which they may not be qualified for acceptance).	Tell them to apply to as many schools as they want whether it is one or twenty, after all, these are their applications. Encourage them to complete many applications, thereby increasing their stress level.
If your teens are having difficulty deciding what school should be on their list encourage them to make a set of pros and cons for each school they are considering in order to narrow the list down.	Dictate the schools to which they should apply. After all, you know which schools would be best. Their input isn't necessary even though they are the ones who will attend.

In this chapter our aim was to clarify the push and pull that defines your teens' march toward adulthood. In the next chapter we address the cycle of lies and secrets which can sometimes veer both you and your teen off course.

LET'S REVIEW: TIPS FOR TRANSLATING

Now that you feel confident about sending your teens on the road to independence, we offer the following as a recap of what you will need to remember as you prepare yourself for their journey.

1. **Autonomy Leads to Independence:** By providing a balance of structure and guidance you encourage your teens to become self-reliant.

2. **Positive Parent–Child Relationships Result in Positive Peer Groups:** Although you may feel as if you have little influence over your teens' choice of friends, if you have a positive relationship with your teens they are more likely to develop positive peer relationships.

3. **Technology Takes It to a Whole New Level:** Social networking tools have created a whole new forum in which teens can get to know each other. Early dating may primarily focus on teens connecting with each other using these tools.

4. **Prescription May Lead to Deception:** Work with your teen to create dating rules and guidelines you both agree upon. Avoid dictating or prescribing specifically who your teen can date as this can lead to noncompliance and sneaking around.

5. **Teach Your Children Well:** The most effective teacher is the one who will remain calm and constructive. By modeling safe driving behavior to your teens you become their greatest resource.

6. **Make Informed Decisions about Your Teens' Driving Practices:** It is important to keep in mind that young drivers are at greatest risk of involvement in fatal car accidents. The majority of such accidents occur when your teens are driving with other teens, driving at night, and/or over the weekend.

7. **Be Informed Not Intrusive:** The process of applying to college can at times seem complicated and confusing. You should offer your teen information in interactive discussions. If your teens' do not demonstrate interest, step back and look for other timely opportunities when the conversations are not too overwhelming.

8. **Offer Aid not Attitude or Authorship:** Your teens may become so overwhelmed by the task of submitting college applications that they have difficulty getting started. It is important for you to allow your teens to negotiate this process. Remain calm and supportive and refrain from organizing or actually completing their applications for them.

CHAPTER 5

Lies and Secrets: Who Is Keeping Whom in the Dark?

A family environment that is characterized by parents who are seen as supportive, available, respectful of feelings, tolerant of mistakes, and capable of forgiveness is likely to lead to the most sincere and honest communication with teens. Study after study bears this out and we would like this to become the style of your family and the climate of your home. A 2006 study published in the *Journal of Youth and Adolescence* found, for example, that kids who lie more often have less trusting relationships with their parents.

Some little white lies may be necessary for everyone. It is, however, the pattern of consistent lying about stressors that we are most concerned about. Interestingly and probably not surprisingly, whether or not your teenagers talk to you is based on whether or not they see you as trustworthy. Parents' ratings of their own trustworthiness are often strikingly different from the ratings of parental trustworthiness by their children. Teenagers view trustworthiness as the ability of their parent to be honest, to look out for their best interests, to keep promises, and to keep what teens have said confidential. So clearly, after your teens open up to you, do not get on the phone and let your teens overhear you divulging what they have just shared; this is a mistake that many parents make. These parents are probably simply trying to get their friends' opinions about their teenagers, but if you lie to your teenagers and break a promise about keeping their secrets, you will create teenagers who not only don't trust you, but who also will put a lot of energy into *not* talking to you.

As you read this chapter bear in mind that we have learned from teens themselves that secrecy, lack of disclosure, and lying may lead to loneliness and even lack of parental involvement. What appears to happen is that the more your teens lie the less you ask. You, like your teens, become avoidant and close the doors of communication even further. In this case, there is little or even no *Teenage* or adult language being used. In addition, teens who lie frequently report lower levels of self-esteem and higher levels of unhappiness and stress. As if that were not enough to convince you of the problems related to lying, teens who lie frequently tend to show more aggression, more impulsivity, and lower levels of self-control. So the takeaway message here is that lying is not healthy for any of us, particularly your teens. The question now becomes, if it's so detrimental then why do they do it? And how can you talk to your teens about lying in general?

To Lie or Not to Lie That Is the Question

Children begin to lie early in life for a variety of reasons. Transgressions and getting into trouble are part of normal childhood behavior. As your kids develop into teenagers their lies are often of greater concern because you rely more on them for your knowledge of what they are doing outside of the home. As we all are aware, it is much easier to know what your young children are doing. You arrange their play dates, know the homes and parents of their friends, and basically monitor many of their daily activities. With teens, this level of monitoring is not recommended, possible, or even likely to result in any kind of positive outcome. Your teens may end conversations abruptly by leaving the house, hanging up the phone, or by refusing to make eye contact. They may act disinterested, or they may change the subject or postpone the discussion (how many times have your teens told you they would talk about something later and here you are reading this still waiting for it to be later!). Finally, your teens may express their discomfort by reacting emotionally, expressing distress, or even crying. Less frequently, your teens may actually listen to what you are saying but offer no response or a simple nod. Sometimes your teens may avoid topics by gently reassuring you that they are making good decisions (which may in fact be true) and that you should not worry about them.

So the question remains why do your teens hold on to secrets and lie? There are many answers including:

1. They are ashamed and embarrassed.
2. They are afraid of getting into trouble.
3. They are afraid that if they tell you, then you might tell everyone.
4. They have observed parents and other adults lying.
5. They lie so you'll think of them as responsible kids and continue to reward them by allowing them to drive the car, letting them go out, give them later curfews, etc.
6. They lie to cover up for friends.
7. Probably more than any other reason, they lie to avoid disapproval from parents. They are afraid that you won't like them anymore.

8. They lie because they don't know how to get out of the mess they've gotten into.

9. They lie to avoid worrying you.

You see the real secret being kept here is how much they care about your approval and support. Lying becomes a part of teenage language and sadly translates into "I am afraid that you will disapprove of me if you really know what I'm up to." This is the real reason beneath the secrets and lies.

Do What I Say Not What I Do?

Lies and secrets usually stem primarily from fear. Your teens face many of the same fears that you currently face or have faced in the past. They are afraid of being embarrassed and of the feelings of shame that follow. Shame is, after all, among the most difficult of feelings to manage. Teens, like adults, are afraid of being judged, criticized, and disliked. They don't want to get into trouble and fear severe punishment and disapproval. After all, who among us has not told something that strays from the truth in an effort to avoid worrying others or to cover up for others?

In order to discourage your teens from lying we encourage you to try the following behaviors:

Role Model Honesty for Your Teens

It is well documented that we learn best by observing others, particularly those that we look up to and from whom we seek approval—such as the way teens look up to and seek approval from adults. It's no surprise that teens sometimes observe adults keeping secrets and lying. As we discussed in Chapter 3, your teens observe you very closely. They often mimic your behavior. When they are in a jam and not sure how to handle it, they think about how you would act in a similar situation. The message here is that you should not underestimate the power of observational learning. Your kids learn not only by what you say, but perhaps even more importantly by what you do.

GET THEM TALKING

"It's not a major issue." "It can stay between us."

If you are able to keep a confidence teens are more likely to actually tell you the whole story.

For example, let's say that you have a friend who you do not wish to speak to in the moment. By taking her phone call and explaining that this is not a good time to talk rather than having your husband lie and say that you are not home, you are modeling honesty in a potentially stressful situation. Likewise, if you as a father are being asked to coach yet another softball team, then go ahead and be honest in explaining that you have too much on your plate and are not available for additional coaching. This honest approach, rather than saying something like "I'll be out of town for the next four weeks" (assuming this is not true), sends your teens the message that you are honest even when you are afraid that you might disappoint someone. Basically, what we are suggesting is that you teach your teens not to lie by being honest to them and to others even if it means having to tolerate uncomfortable feelings. You want to model honesty *not* avoidance.

We also suggest not lying *for* your teens in an effort to protect them. If they have gotten themselves into a difficult situation encourage them to find a way to deal. By being honest in most situations, particularly those in which it would be easier to lie, you teach your teens that being honest is more important than being avoidant and that over time you yourself have learned to deal with anxiety-provoking situations with an honest approach. Sometimes it's very tempting to help your stressed kids by telling a white lie, but the problem with this is twofold. In these situations you not only teach that lying is acceptable but you also prevent your teens from learning the skills necessary to work their way out of difficult situations. There are many examples of this in everyday life. Your teen may ask you to say that he is not home when he receives a phone call that he'd rather not take. Perhaps, it would be a better idea to encourage him to deal with this phone call directly. The same teen may not want to write an essay due tomorrow and may ask you to write a note with a phony excuse such as "Steven was ill last night. Please give him an extension on his assignment," or even "Emma's cousins were visiting from out of town this weekend so please excuse her from the report that was due today." Do you recognize yourself in some of the above examples? We are not trying to make you feel guilty or embarrass you. We assume that you were simply trying to reduce your children's stress levels. However, although you may be reducing your teens' stress levels in the short-run by lying for them, you may inadvertently be depriving them of developing coping skills and teaching them that lying is an appropriate behavior at the same time.

OKAY:

1. An expression that states agreement.

PARENT: "Will you drive your sister home tomorrow?"

TEENAGER: "Okay."

SUGGESTED PARENTAL RESPONSE: "Thank you." Your teen is being helpful and mature.

2. A comment that reflects an attempt to end the conversation.

PARENT: "Would you please do that already? I've asked you ten times."

TEENAGER: "Okay!"

SUGGESTED PARENTAL RESPONSE: Back off! It sounds like you are both getting annoyed.

Remain Calm and Involved with Your Teens Even When You Begin to Feel Emotional

If your teens come to talk to you about a potentially embarrassing behavior, try very hard not to display your feelings. Your teens will undoubtedly feel more inclined to honestly confide if they believe that you can handle things in a relaxed manner. If they are used to you becoming emotionally overwhelmed and being ruled by your emotions then they are much more likely to lie to you. They are not lying to you because they are bad kids but rather because they are afraid of upsetting you and stressing you out, and probably don't know how to act in response to you becoming overwhelmed by emotions. Teens have enough difficulty dealing with their own emotions; you certainly can't expect them to know how to deal with an emotionally overwhelmed parent. We also encourage you to try to remain calm because you will think more clearly and be a better responder and problem-solver when you are not feeling emotionally charged. Who among us has not regretted saying something unkind in an emotional moment?

I LOVE YOU:

1. A statement of genuine affection.
PARENT: "I am so happy for you."
TEENAGER: "I love you."
SUGGESTED PARENTAL RESPONSE: Smile. Be happy. You are loved!

2. An expression used to convey that your teens are displeased and not surprised by the response that you gave them.
PARENT: "No, I am not going to make your curfew later."
TEENAGER: "I love you."
SUGGESTED PARENTAL RESPONSE: NONE. You have made your point. No need to get into a struggle.

Instead of becoming emotional, try to minimize rather than escalate their anxiety levels. If, for example, they confide to you that they are being teased, help them understand that you support and respect them regardless of what their peers are saying. By all means, stay calm and listen—and read Chapter 7 to learn more about how to deal with bullying. In an emotionally relaxed state, perhaps you can help them brainstorm ways to handle the teasing.

Work with Them to Devise Consequences That Match Their Misdeeds

At times, your teens will confide in you and you will need to be both nurturing and deliver consequences. Although we encourage you to be calm when your teens confide in you, this does not rule out providing the necessary and hopefully previously agreed upon consequences. If you consistently deliver very harsh consequences then your teens will be more likely to be secretive and lie. They will do this in an effort to avoid the restrictive consequences. A harsh consequence, for example, would be one month of grounding for skipping one class. As discussed in Chapter 1, consequences should be consistent with the misdeed.

Remember, the goal of consequences is not to destroy your teens' self-esteem or to ruin their social lives. It is simply to help teach them that, at home, as in life in general, there are natural consequences for unacceptable behavior. As discussed in Chapter 1, the best way to determine consequences and to teach your teens self-control is by working with them to create a list of rules and corresponding fair and reasonable consequences prior to the occurrence of negative behaviors. The hope is that your teens will internalize expectations within themselves and will arrive at a point where they are able to differentiate acceptable from unacceptable behavior on their own. This is why it is so important that you are consistent in following through on the assigned consequences. Next time your teens think about engaging in the same misdeed, they will remember that there will be a consequence for them to deal with.

Avoid Divulging Their Secrets, If Possible

There are times when it will be difficult to keep their stories between the two of you, but we recommend that you try to provide a trustworthy and respectful family environment by treating their stories like precious information. Sometimes this will take a lot of self-control on your part. After all, it is a human tendency to want to bounce information off of your friends and relatives. However, honoring your child's wishes should be your first priority.

For example, if your teen tells you that they a have a crush on someone, we suggest that you keep this harmless information to yourself. You have the option of potentially embarrassing your teen by announcing or blurting this information to their siblings. Doing so will almost guarantee that the child who shared information with you will be reluctant to do so in the future. Doesn't this make sense to you? Remember back to your teen years. Wouldn't you have cringed and shut down if your father told your brothers that you had recently confided that you had a crush on one of their friends? We certainly expect that you would have been deeply embarrassed.

At times, it is not even beneficial to share their stories with others. If, for example, your teen confides in you that she accidentally broke your necklace rather than lost it, then this is likely not something that you need to share with others. You want to avoid shaming your child. If, however, your teens confide in you about something that you feel you must share with others, we suggest that you tell them in advance.

The goal is to always maintain a good quality relationship characterized by honesty and good modeling. For example, if your teen tells you that he was the one who banged up your partner's car, then this is the type of confidence that you need to share. You have several options here: One option is that you can tell your teen that you will tell his father; or you can encourage your teen to tell his father, directly, by himself; or, finally, you can offer to be present and provide loving support while your teen tells the truth to his father. We prefer the second and third options because they encourage the development of skill building. In these instances, you will teach your teens that facing situations that make them anxious can actually lead to developing confidence in their abilities to handle such situations smoothly and with positive outcomes.

If you and your teen decide on the third and final option we urge you to be present in a silent but supportive manner and let your teen and your partner work out the situation. You are not there to be a buffer or mediator. You are also not there to protect your child. Be sure to let your teen know that you are simply there to provide a supportive presence. We also recommend that you not tell your partner in advance. We know that you mean well, but often naturally occurring situations provide your teen with the best learning opportunities. Telling your partner will defeat the purpose of your teen and your partner managing and dealing with their natural reactions to one another. You also don't want to give your teen the message that he is incapable of handling the situation on his own. A good rule of thumb to keep in mind throughout your children's lives is that if you handle most stressful situations for them then you are sending the message that you doubt their capabilities. This is one message that you certainly do not want to send. Try to replace it with "I believe in you."

We want to make it clear here that we are not encouraging you to keep secrets that might be harmful if kept private; we are instead asking you to use common sense when deciding what to share. A good question for you to ask yourself is: "Would anyone face harm if I maintained my child's confidence?" If the answer is "No," then you show your teen that your are trustworthy by keeping the harmless information private. If the answer is "Yes," and you keep the secret, then you run the risk of modeling bad judgment. If, however, the answer is "Yes" and you are going to share the secret with someone else, then we advise you to tell your child in a loving and supportive manner why it is necessary to betray her trust. She may not be pleased but at least you will have attempted to clarify why you are doing what you feel needs to be done.

Try to Avoid Belittling and Critical Responses

This is a good bit of wisdom to follow in most life situations but is particularly important with your developing teens. We suggest that when your teens confide in you that you treat them with empathy, honor, and dignity simply because they are your children. We believe that this is the best style to use in your family and in your life in general. It is the style that will send the message that you are a parent to be trusted, respected, and to come to when they are in confusing situations. Think about it. If you had the choice of confiding in a friend who told you that you "Blew it," or a friend who told you that "We all make mistakes," who would you choose to talk to? You are also teaching your teens kind, tolerant, and nonjudgmental behavior by avoiding a critical style. In the event that your teen is being bullied, you certainly don't want to give her the message that you are in agreement with the bullies by being critical of her. Sometimes, parents do this without even realizing it. By saying something like "I can't believe you let her get away with saying that to you" or "You are too sensitive," you unintentionally give your child the message that you agree with the bullies. Now, what parent actually intends to send such a devastating message? Again, more on bullying in Chapter 7.

PAT ON YOUR BACK:

1. A small gesture of appreciation.
PARENT: "You did a nice job."
TEENAGER: Pats you on your back.
SUGGESTED PARENTAL RESPONSE: Smile. Your teen appreciates your support.

2. A gesture indicating that your teen thinks that you are clueless.
PARENT: "That girl next door gets all A's and probably never gets into trouble."
TEENAGER: Pats you on your back.
SUGGESTED PARENTAL RESPONSE: Hmm. Perhaps you should rethink this opinion. No further comment is necessary at this point.

Find Opportunities to Praise Your Teens

If you create an atmosphere where only the most successful behaviors are praised then your teens are likely to keep secrets from you when they feel that they have disappointed you. They may even begin to lie about grades and social status if they feel that you will only praise them or reward them for the very best behavior. This is particularly true if you have a tendency to compare them to their higher-achieving and more popular siblings and friends. We suggest withholding criticism, not praise. You want your teens to feel that you are members and leaders of their fan club. They have plenty of places outside of the home where they don't get praise.

GET THEM TALKING

"I love your boots. What did your friends say about them?"
You can expect your teens to talk about the boots and then start talking about their day. Try to avoid yes/no questions.

Keep in mind that children of all ages and especially teens are less likely to lie if they perceive their family environment as supportive, respectful, and tolerant of mistakes. We suggest creating a family atmosphere where to the best of your ability, you honor and praise all of your children, simply because they are your children. If you tune in when they speak, listen to them when they are attempting to express feelings, and avoid ignoring them when they are speaking their teenage language, either verbal or nonverbal, then you will surely hear something worthy of praise. If possible, praise the way that they are thinking about things, praise their problem solving skills, and certainly praise any displays of empathy or kindness that they discuss. Watch your teens carefully and you will find many, many behaviors to praise. Watch how they treat their friends, siblings, pets, etc. Watch how they try so hard to do so many things well. The more you watch, the more you'll notice praiseworthy behaviors. Without overdoing it, praise your teens at every possible opportunity. Teens who live in an environment of love, acceptance, and appreciation are the least likely to lie to you. They know that you basically think well of them and know that you expect missteps at times.

Befriend Your Teens' Friends

Criticizing their teens' friends is probably one of the worst mistakes that parents make. There is a natural tendency to protect your children and sometimes this translates into the language of criticism of their friends. What you fail to realize, however, is that by criticizing your teens' friends you are in a sense criticizing your own children. Teens identify intensely with their friends. By saying, for example, "I'm not sure that I like your friend Emma. I don't know what it is about her," you are, in effect, criticizing your own teen's judgment and her sense of identity. Unless you have reason to suspect that your teens' friends are involved in serious acting-out behaviors, such as drug involvement, we recommend that you keep your feelings to yourself. If you are nonjudgmental and accepting of your teens' friends then they will be more likely to seek your advice when their friends are in tricky or difficult situations. They are also less likely to lie to cover up for friends because they expect your support rather than your critiques!

When we say that you should befriend your teen's friends we do not mean that you should begin to act like a teenager. We mean, instead, that you should make an effort to be friendly and kind to your teens' friends. Make an effort to speak their language. This means getting to know them by asking about their interests and talking to them about topics that are appropriate and low key. You may be lucky if your house becomes the one at which the teens feel comfortable gathering. This will provide you with an excellent opportunity to get to know your teens' friends even better. There will then be fewer opportunities for your kids to lie since they know that you are in an excellent position to hear the truth from their friends. So, in an effort to prevent lying, get friendly with the kids who may have the real story!

Provide Opportunities for Your Teens to Earn Rewards

We know that teens sometimes lie about their behaviors so that they will avoid losing out on rewards such as the use of the car, a sleepover, a later curfew, allowance, or perhaps even a new guitar. They are afraid that if you knew the truth about their poor grades, study habits, and mean behaviors toward their siblings, etc., that they would not earn these privileges. In fact, they are probably right. If you were aware of such misbehavior then you would very likely not provide rewards and privileges.

In an effort to make it unnecessary for your teens to lie in order to earn rewards, we suggest that you develop a system of clearly linked behaviors and privileges; and that you collaborate with your teens about the ways they can earn rewards. If, for example, your child does his chores and his homework, then perhaps he can earn money toward his new guitar. Of course, if you find out that he has been bullying his younger brother into doing the chores for him, then you have a different situation on which to focus. If your daughter's grades have been deteriorating, then maybe you'd like to see a three point increase in her Spanish average before you allow her to have her next sleepover. If your other teenager has been tutoring her younger brother in math, perhaps she can earn a manicure or some other type of special treatment as a reward for her helpfulness.

GET THEM TALKING

"How many girls/boys showed up for the party?"

After answering, your teens may actually start talking about the party.

We encourage parents to be careful not to set up a system of expectations that are unreasonable or too difficult for their teens to meet. It's also important to recognize the unique abilities of each of your teens and to reward effort, good teamwork, and achievement accordingly. These are all valuable skills that benefit us in our daily lives. The goal is for your teens to earn rewards through their successes rather than from avoidance or lying. Always remember, that the majority of your teens would much rather struggle to please you then lie to you and disappoint you.

Keep Your Secrets to Yourself—What They Do Know Can Hurt Them!

As a parent, you may now be very confused. We have suggested that you consistently model honesty for your teens. We would like to qualify this by explaining that there are some very sensitive topics that are better dealt with by not discussing them at all or by discussing them in a very careful manner.

Studies have repeatedly shown that parents are ill-advised to disclose too much negative personal information to their teens. Adolescents tend to show signs of distress, emotional upset, and worry when parents use them as confidantes to whom they confide their worry, anger, and complaints. They also do not benefit from being asked to give you advice about personal matters. This, too, leads them to feel anxious, worried, and at times confused about their roles with you. Again, we are not encouraging lying. There are some topics, however, that are more appropriate to discuss with adult friends and/or support group members. When in doubt, ask yourself how you felt or would feel when and if your own parents discussed such information with you.

Always keep in mind that your teens are your children, not your friends, no matter how mature they may appear. Teens are not ready or emotionally equipped to deal with some of the information that you may be tempted to tell them. Remember their age and child status even though they may listen and not show signs of distress in the moment. To this end avoid discussing these sensitive topics:

1. *Criticizing their parent from whom you are divorced.* This can only lead to negative outcomes. This may result not only in a lower quality of relationship with the other parent but may also strain your own relationships with your teens. Do you admire people who constantly devalue and criticize others? Criticizing others often backfires.

2. *Your dating troubles or requesting dating advice.* Although you may be tempted to get advice from your teens please resist. We

can assure you that this topic will not only make them uncomfortable but may also make them feel queasy. Teens are very uncomfortable thinking about their parents outside of the role of "the parent." We are not suggesting that you not date. We are advising, instead, that you get your dating advice from more appropriate listeners.

3. *Marital problems.* Teens are very sensitive. They are probably painfully aware of your marital tensions and are attempting to deal with them in their own ways. By all means, do not use them as your confidantes in these stressful situations. They will resent you for involving them in adult issues. In addition, they will worry and may be prevented from developing the right level of emotional distance and autonomy that they so badly need to develop at this age.

4. *Extramarital affairs.* If you are involved in an affair this is clearly not an issue to share with your teens. If you choose, nonetheless, to confide you will not only teach them that secret keeping and cheating are okay, but you will also put them in a tricky relationship with their other parent. They will resent you for this.

5. *Chronic complaining and anger.* Your teens look at you and think "Is this what it's like to grow older?" If you confide your discontent to your teens then they are likely to avoid you, and you, in turn, are likely to avoid them. You do not want to create a cycle of avoidance. Complain and express your frustrations about your life to either your friends, coworkers, parents, or a professional. In other words, confide in someone who is in a position to advise you.

6. *Secrets about other family members.* Do not put your teens in a position where they know information that they are not supposed to know. Breaking a confidence does not win you points or lead to a better relationship with your teens. What it does instead is send the message that you are not to be trusted with confidential information.

The above list is, of course, not exhaustive. The message is that your teens are not your confidantes. They want you to be the parents and they are certainly not emotionally equipped to provide advice to you. There are times, though, that you may not be sure if your teens are comfortable with the topic at hand. If you are unsure we recommend considering two major sources. First, ask yourself how you would feel or have felt when and if your own parents discussed such stressful issues with you. Second, if your teens are not verbalizing distress, observe their nonverbal behavior (see Chapter 3). There is always the possibility that they will tell you that they are uncomfortable. In our experience, however, we have found that teens are not inclined to be so straightforward. After all, remember, they do not want to upset you and/or let you down. Therefore, you may need to pay attention to their body language for clues of their discomfort.

Masking—When How They Appear Is Not How They Feel

By now you may be feeling more confident about your ability to understand and read what your teens are really saying to you. There is one phenomenon, however, that certainly bears explanation. The teens we have worked with refer to it as masking. Masking occurs when your teens outwardly act as if they feel one way but, in reality, feel differently inside. We all experience times when we feign our feelings. The difficulty is that many teens get so good at masking that it almost becomes an art form.

IGNORING AND/OR AVOIDING YOU:

1. A signal that your teen is deeply immersed in an activity (such as homework).
PARENT: "I have an interesting story to tell you."
TEENAGER: Ignores you and avoids engaging in conversation.
SUGGESTED PARENTAL RESPONSE: "When you're not busy, let's talk."

2. A signal that your teenager is preoccupied with something that may be upsetting him.
PARENT: "Is there something that you would like to tell me about?"
TEENAGER: Ignores you and avoids answering.
SUGGESTED PARENTAL RESPONSE: "Well, if you change your mind, I'd love to hear about what's going on in your life."

For example, think of a time when you took your teens someplace that they seemed to enjoy. Maybe it was a family vacation or a day trip to a cultural event. Your memory of this outing is pleasurable because you recall that even your teens seemed to have a good time. One day you may be talking to a friend who is asking for advice about fun places to take her family. You suggest this place because as you relate to your friend "The whole family had such a wonderful time." Your teens then blurt out "We hated that trip!" You are dumbfounded.

Perhaps masking is revealed when you are asking your son to practice piano or for your daughter to get ready for soccer practice. In the heat of their resistance, they tell you that they do not like piano or soccer; they just do these activities because they seem so important to you. (To you? As if you enjoy driving your kids from activity to activity, racing around like you are a NASCAR driver?) You do it because you love them and these activities make them happy . . . or so you thought. By now you clearly get the picture, but how does masking come about?

In Chapter 1 we introduced you to the *ESP Factor*—the concept that your teens believe you always know what they are thinking, sometimes even before they do. As a result of the *ESP Factor*, your teens assume you can *always* read their mind. When your reaction suggests that you can't, you are likely to get varying responses. A common reaction from a teen when she reveals her true feelings may be a statement like this "You don't know me at all." This can feel very painful. You may want to respond with a hurtful comment. *Please* do not, you will regret it. Both masking and the *ESP Factor* may lead to communication problems and misunderstandings. In addition, kids sometimes mask because they think that you can read their real thoughts and feelings.

You may be scratching your head wondering why teens mask. The answers vary. Teens sometimes do this to appear socially correct. At other times they do so because they think that they are acting the way you want them to act and they want to please you. The teens we have worked with have also told us that they use masking as a coping skill. It is easier to deny their true feelings to the outside world than to deal with the reactions to the way they really feel. Some teens get so good at masking that they themselves report that they are not really sure how they truly feel. At the extreme, masking can be used to hide intense feelings such as depression or anger. As we highlight throughout this book, the best way to address masking is to capitalize on opportunities. The next time your teens reveal that they are not feeling the way they are projecting they are feeling about a situation or event, take note. Wait to approach the topic with them at a later time when things are calm and relaxed. In a caring and concerned manner communicate to them that you were surprised that you misread their feelings. Be sure to point out what their outward appearances suggested. Discuss ways to avoid this in the future. One suggested rule (as noted earlier) is that they agree to *say what they mean and mean what they say*. Explain to them that they are so good at hiding what they really feel that you can't even tell the truth. One tool that sometimes helps is to set up a structured communication system using the *Feeling and Action Scale* that we detailed in Chapter 1; after all, it's a lot easier to say one number than having to go into a detailed explanation. We suggest this scale because often teens will mask because they don't want to deal with possibly negative reactions to their true feelings. It is important to explain to your teens that, while their honest expression of feelings is valued, negative expressions will not and cannot always be met with immediate action (e.g., leaving in the middle of a movie that they find boring). Be prepared that when this is explained your teens may counter by expressing concern. They may tell you that if they can't be accommodated immediately then there is no point to honestly report their feelings. Take this opportunity to explain that how they are feeling is important to you and let them know that although you cannot always provide instant resolution to negative feelings, you want to help them cope with these feelings.

One word of caution, if you are still convinced that the best course of action would be to simply help your teens exit situations which result in negative feelings, be forewarned that you are creating a dynamic which could be troublesome. In life there will be situations that you cannot leave just because you are unhappy, for example, being on an airplane or bus. We think you get the point.

We have provided you with important information regarding honesty, secrets, and lies. We believe this information is essential in discussing the changing roles of parents and redefinitions of the family we present in the next chapter.

LET'S REVIEW: TIPS FOR TRANSLATING

You have now learned the keys to ensuring that you and your teen can communicate with each other in caring and honest ways. To sum up:

1. **Create a Family Environment Where Honesty Is the Best Policy:** A home in which parents are supportive, available, and loving is a home that is likely to have teens who are willing to risk being honest.

2. **Shame and Disapproval Equal Lies and Deceit:** We suggest that you never underestimate how important your approval is to your teens. Although they are not likely to show it, they lie mostly to maintain your approval.

3. **Empathy Equals Understanding:** Empathy will go very far. Although you may need to enforce consequences for misbehavior, remember that no one is perfect and that we all learn from mistakes.

4. **Model Honesty:** Your teens learn much from watching you. Avoid lying to others and for your teens.

5. **Do Not Tell Them Everything:** Refrain from sharing inappropriate subject matters with your teens. Use other members of your support system for this purpose.

6. **Be Equally Available to Listen to Both Their Successes and Failures:** Establish a family environment that both

acknowledges and expects teens to do well at times and not so well at other times. You want a family climate that does not foster shame.

7. **What You See May Not Be How They Feel:** Teens sometimes use masking, which is when teens outwardly present themselves as feeling one way (e.g., happy or accepting) when they really may be feeling another way.

8. **Explain That They Need to "Say What They Mean, and Mean What They Say":** Remind your teens that you do not have ESP and that you want to know how they are really feeling.

CHAPTER 6

The Evolving Identities of Fathers and Mothers: How Traditions Have Been Broken and the Rules about Roles Rewritten

Over the past fifty years the roles of mothers and fathers have evolved. This evolution has blurred the solid lines once drawn to delineate the traditional roles assigned to each parent. As a result, more mothers are not only working outside of the home but are developing and advancing in careers once reserved for men. More fathers are entering fields traditionally reserved for women and because many of these professions offer flexible scheduling (kindergarten teacher) or shift work (nursing), many fathers now have more time to spend at home with their families. In addition, while more moms are choosing to return to work after the birth of their children more fathers are taking paternity leave and/or assuming the responsibilities of the primary caretaker of the children and the home.

Technology has also contributed to these changing roles. Many of you are now able to telecommute allowing you to perform a majority of work tasks using technology at home. The benefits of this new approach to working are many. Precious time once dedicated to traveling to and from the workplace can now be reinvested in the family, allowing you to participate and enjoy more of your teens' lives than ever before. And, in many cases, office-less jobs have also provided you with the opportunity to create more flexible work schedules. This means that even if you are the main breadwinner, you are no longer an absent provider but an active participant in daily family life. There has also been a steady increase in home-based self-employment. Burgeoning fields such as technology and the service industry have afforded many parents the opportunity to set up shop within the comfort of their own homes.

In addition, the composition of the average family has also changed. Due to the high divorce rate, the traditional nuclear family has been redesigned and reorganized. Blended families (the combining of two families as the result of remarriage) have practically become the norm rather than the exception. Stepparents have been incorporated into the family structure. Emerging new definitions of parenting roles present families with questions of who should parent, when, how, and how much.

Overall, these changes can be positive for most families. Changes however, rarely come without challenges. If you have recently made one of these changes you may be scratching your head as to why the transition has been more difficult for you and your teens than you had originally imagined. You may be experiencing some of the issues that often arise in these less-traditional arrangements. Here, we will emphasize how communicating with your teens to create guidelines and discuss adjustments can ensure an environment that is both peaceful and productive.

Breaking with Tradition: Reassigning and Reorganizing Parenting Roles

There are many changes and scenarios that can shape each parent's role in the household. The impact of these changes on any given household will depend on the situation. Economic trends often dictate an individual family's circumstances. If, for example, you have decided to take on the role of stay-at-home parent due to a job layoff, both you and your teens may need to adjust to the situation.

Perhaps you and your partner are nurses working opposite shifts. This arrangement has worked well over the years—until recently that is. You have both noted consistent objections from your teens such as "Mom let's me when she is home," or "That's not how dad does it." Maybe you are a professional who looks forward to assuming the role of mom or dad as soon as you walk in the door. There is only one problem: As your kids have gotten older, they seem less available and sometimes you feel as if they don't even realize you have come home. Long gone are the days when your son or daughter ran to give you a big hug at the door; even the dog seems less enthusiastic when greeting you (okay he's fourteen years old but still!). Perhaps you are parenting in a dual-earner home. While both you and our partner are successful at work, you struggle to maintain the balance at home. After all, you both work hard all day, aren't your teens old enough to understand that when you come home you just want everyone to get along? Why do they seem so demanding one moment and so distant the next? It is with these circumstances in mind that we offer the suggestions and guidelines in the following table to help ensure that you can feel successful in communicating with your teens at home—regardless of your job title.

TRY THIS	RATHER THAN THIS
If your parenting role will be changing in the near future engage your teens in an interactive discussion about these changes. Encourage them to provide input regarding how or if they believe the changes will impact them. Discuss your own perspectives.	Your teens don't need to know if there will be changes that may affect them. They will just have to deal with the situation when it arises. Who cares what they think? After all, you are the parent and they will do what you tell them.
Make sure that everyone understands and accepts the household rules (see Chapter 1 for guidelines on the rule-making process). You and your partner need to present a unified front. Any rule changes or additions should be discussed together.	Each parent dictates their own set of rules when they are the one in charge. Who cares if there are contradictions?
All family members should use the Feeling and Action Scale (see Chapter 1). This is an especially useful way for those of you who are working parents to ensure that your teens don't blame themselves for the impact work-related stress may have on you on any given day.	You don't need to justify your bad moods. If you are in a bad mood everyone should just leave you alone!
You and your partner should check in with each other. If one of you is feeling stressed or overwhelmed, the other needs to step in and take over. Give each other a break and share the responsibilities together. This response can prevent negative mood–based interactions between you and your teens. By watching out for each other you and your partner also model to your teens what a loving and caring partnership should look like.	Ignore your partner's negative moods. If your partner is behaving badly toward you or your teens, yell at your partner in front of the kids.

Who's Minding the Kids?—The Particular Dilemmas of the Dual-Earner Household

If both you and your partner work, you are probably all too familiar with stressors related to raising teenagers in a dual-earner household. Whether you have both always worked, or whether one of you has decided to go back to work now that the kids are older, you face a set of challenges unique to your situation. Thankfully there has been a sharp increase in the number and types of safe and creative childcare options available to today's working parents. As children get older, however, these options shrink and now that your kids have reached their teens you may be faced with a dilemma. Even if you could find a babysitter or nanny to be at home for your teens, unless they are there under the guise that they are watching younger siblings, we can almost guarantee that once your teens attend high school, the sitter will no longer be accepted. How do you affirm your teen's autonomy and independence while ensuring their safety—and your sanity? We offer the following guidelines to help you out.

Create a Consistent Daily Check-In Plan

Require your teens to contact you at the same time every day just to check in. This interaction should be brief. As we have already discussed, too many questions are likely to be perceived as an interrogation and will shut your teens down. Follow their lead and keep the conversation light. If they take it someplace else (e.g., talk about a concern at school that day) go with it. Listen and respond appropriately. We suggest that you require a phone call instead of a text message so the contact is more personal. However, if you know both you and your spouse will not be able to talk one day due to work-related duties, then have your teens text instead of call; after all, some contact is better than none. If possible, ensure that the schedule for this contact includes both you and your partner. Alternate days between yourselves if this works better. When both of you are involved it demonstrates that you are both equally invested in your teens.

Know Your Teens' Daily Schedule

This is especially important if your teens are involved in several after-school activities such as sports teams or clubs. Arrange a time with your teens to quickly go through what their schedules will look like for the week. This will provide you with important information regarding the locations of your teens and will keep you informed about how they are spending their days. This sends the message that your teens' time is just as important to you as yours. Keeping informed will also provide you with opportunities to communicate with your teens about their interests and concerns.

If Your Teens Will Require Transportation to After-School Activities, Work Out a Plan in Advance

Nothing is more stressful than scrambling around at the last minute to find your teens a ride to a practice or an after-school lesson. In addition, they may believe that because you have waited for the last minute to devise a plan, you do not really care about what is important to them and that making arrangements to get them to their activities is merely an afterthought in your busy life. Turn to your friends for help or work out deals with other involved parents so that you can do your fair share. If, for example, practices are during the week and the weekend, offer to transport regularly during the times you are available. Even if other parents offer to take on the full responsibility it is important to do your share. By doing what you can, you demonstrate to your teens that their activities are important. If your older teens are driving your younger children to their activities, refer to Chapter 4 for some cautions regarding this arrangement.

Switch Off with Your Partner to Attend Any of Your Teens' Games, Performances, or Presentations That Take Place During Work Hours

It may sometimes feel as though you are the only dual-earner family! Why do schools schedule so many important events during the day? Even if your teens tell you they don't care if you cannot attend any of their games or performances, our experience is that the *ESP Factor* is really at work. To translate: Your teens usually do want you there and they make the assumption that you know how important these events are to them and will find a way to show up.

Perhaps your teens are not directly impacted by your inability to attend any of these events, but they may be indirectly affected. Do you want to be the parent of the teens that no one has ever seen or met? Believe us, people talk, and unfortunately your teens are listening. If neither you nor your partner can attend, try to have a relative or friend to whom your teens feel close attend. Of course there may be times when attendance is just not possible. Sit down and explain this to you teens. Assure them that while they are more important than your work, unfortunately, you must sometimes choose the latter.

Hats Off to Single Working Parents

Most of what we have presented above also applies to single working parents. However, we do realize there are unique challenges faced by those of you who are parenting alone. In the most optimal situation, you may have an amicable relationship with your teens' other parent and, although one of you may be considered the custodial parent, both of you make decisions about your kids together. If you reside close to each other then we recommend that you follow the suggestions we have offered above. If, however, you are a single parent who is going it alone we do offer some additional helpful hints.

Develop a Reliable Support Network

A reliable support network is important for so many reasons. In addition to providing you with a group of confidantes, a role you should not put your teens in (see Chapters 5 and 7), a support network provides you with people to turn to when you need help or back-up. It is important that your teens are well acquainted with your supporters. This way they will feel comfortable if and when you need to send someone else to pick them up or even cheer them on if you are unable to do so. Make sure to talk to your teens about why you rely on this group. Above all, whenever possible inform your teens when you will ask one of your supporters to step in for you. You do not want to catch them off guard. This can sometimes result in annoyance and even anger from them.

Sometimes You Can't Do It All

By acknowledging your limitations, you create opportunities to work with your teens to problem solve. There will be times when your teens will be impacted by your inability to cover all bases. Conceptualize these situations as opportunities to show your teens how to manage disappointment—an important skill for them to hone. If you make it your practice to instantly meet all of your teens' needs despite your own personal consequences you also run the risk of burning yourself out, which is a situation that is not good for you or your teens.

Make Useful Connections to Help You Negotiate Systems

In addition to establishing a support network, with a little ingenuity you can get information regarding your teens by making appropriate connections. If, for example, you want to arrange your work schedule to catch some of your teens' games this season, contact the school athletics department or the assistant coach or coach several weeks before the season begins to find out about the scheduling. Game schedules are usually planned way in advance. Or if your teens are late dialing in for their after-school check-in call one day, do not panic. A quick call to the school district transportation department to determine if buses are running on schedule can be helpful. In some cases you may even be able to find out whether your teens have already been dropped off. We are not suggesting that you do this behind your teens' backs. While it may annoy them that you are collecting this information, explain to them that it helps you manage your own stress regarding their well-being in ways besides asking them a lot of questions.

"Hey Kids, We're Home—For Good": How Telecommuting and Home-Based Businesses Are Changing the Definitions of Parenting

If you are currently telecommuting or are self-employed in a home-based business, you are no doubt benefiting from the greater flexibility and the lack of a commute. However, you may already be faced with several challenges you hadn't considered when you first decided that your home would be your office. In the following table we discuss these challenges and concerns and offer some solutions.

HOW YOU SEE IT	HOW THEY SEE IT
Whenever you are on an important business call your teens seem to require your attention.	You are always on the phone. It is hard to tell which call is more important than the next. Your teens wouldn't be bothering you unless it was important.
You need your teens to respect your work hours and work space. If you worked in an offsite office they would not just barge in whenever they felt like it.	Sometimes it feels as if their parents are always working. It is hard to know when they can talk to their parents and when they can't. Besides, they always knock before they enter their parents' at-home offices.
It is difficult to get work done when your teens are making so much noise. Don't they understand this is your work and it is important that you are able to have an environment in which you can be productive?	This is your teens' house too. Your teens work hard all day at school and practice, they want to unwind and just be themselves. If they are making too much noise, maybe you could find another place to work.
You are so excited about working from home. Now you can spend more time with your teens. Why is it that they seem so annoyed when you try to interact with them when they get home or join in conversations when they bring friends home after school?	Your teens love you, but it feels like now that you are working from home you are always around. It can get annoying when you jump in when they bring friends home.

Of course by now you realize that the best way to address these issues is through direct communication with your teens. By working to establish guidelines that address your teens' concerns, you can ensure that both you and your teens reap only the benefits from your home-based work situation. We offer the following suggestions:

- *Establish a designated space for yourself.* A separate room that serves as your home office is optimal. If space is an issue in your home, an area in a lesser used room (such as your bedroom) will do.
- *Develop a system of signals that indicate if and when you are available.* A shut office door, for example, can mean that no one is to bother you. A two-sided sign on the door like the ones used in hotels can also be useful. If you are in an open space, develop a system of hand signals that indicate whether you are available.
- *Clearly define your work hours.* This is not only important for your teens but for you as well. The most common complaint of individuals working from home is that the work day never ends. It is important to set limits. If you are working your schedule around family responsibilities, for example, taking a break to go to your teen's game, make sure to communicate this. If your schedule is variable, develop a daily schedule and post it in a common area (e.g., on the refrigerator).
- *Establish a way your teens can communicate with you while you are working.* A dry erase board on your office door can be useful, or a text or call on your cell phone. Remember if you were working in an office they would still be able to reach you. Have a discussion regarding when/how you can respond to their needs. It is

challenging for your teens to see you or know that you are home, but not have your attention when they want it.

- *Respect your teens' space.* If you have recently started working at home, remember that while you may be overjoyed to be around your teens more often, you do not want your enthusiasm to be perceived as intrusive. Your teens need to get used to having you around more. They have probably developed a routine and are not used to disruptions. Remember, your teens work hard all day, they have probably gotten used to the calm and quiet that comes with an empty house. You will all need some time to get adjusted.

How the Roles Within the Typical Family Have Become Atypical

The typical American family characterized by Norman Rockwell in his famous paintings has been through a vibrant metamorphosis over the last several decades. Were Rockwell to depict today's version of the family, we expect there would be many more participants sitting at the table including parents, stepparents, stepchildren, and half brothers and sisters, just to name a few. This updated version of the family commonly involves several more personalities with whom to interact and new roles to define. Effective communication is the key to avoiding conflict and encouraging harmony within the home. Below we offer a set of general guidelines we recommend to help all families achieve this end:

1. *The blending of a family should be part of a process, not a discrete event.* It goes without saying that stepchildren who are going to live together should be well acquainted before the day of

the wedding! Keep your teens informed of the status of a serious relationship. Of course we are not suggesting that you give them a play by play of your romantic life. However, we are suggesting that you prepare them as much as possible if you believe that you may be taking a current relationship to a level that will directly impact them such as getting married or moving in together. Listen to their thoughts and feelings. Be honest about what, if any, impact their opinions will have on your decisions. Do not get discouraged. Even with the best efforts, it takes time for everyone to adjust to a new family situation, especially teens.

2. *Conceptualize the blended family as a distinct family unit.* The Brady Bunch may have presented a seemingly unattainable ideal of the blended family. You will recall, however, that the Brady's saw their blended family as a unique whole. In an effort to work together as a family, it is important to acknowledge yourselves as a family. Avoid characterizing yourselves as pieces of other families. Work together to create a set of family rules and guidelines.

3. *Clearly define and acknowledge the value of each family member's role.* This will encourage all family members to think of themselves and the others as being one part of an important whole. It is both comforting and empowering to feel part of something greater.

When families are blended the special role of stepparents often comes to the forefront. In an effort to acknowledge this we offer a separate section devoted to this role.

Stepparents: Shaking the Cinderella Complex

With a high divorce rate and a high rate of remarriage, more and more people are finding themselves with more roles to fill including ex-partner, new parent, and stepparent. And there is no doubt that stepparents play an increasingly important role in the lives of teenagers. Under the right circumstances, stepparents can contribute to the overall well-being of their teenage stepchildren. However, we would like to acknowledge that almost all families go through a difficult and challenging time in the process of reorganization and filling their new roles. In fact, we feel that it is safe to say that there is invariably a period of great turmoil before the new family settles down into new, more relaxed and comfortable patterns. But it is important to keep in mind that a positive relationship between a stepparent and stepchild is related to the overall well-being of the entire family.

So, the ideas that we propose for fostering a good relationship between you and your adolescent stepchildren should result in a win–win situation where everyone is relatively content. A 2009 study suggests that you may be even more sensitive to conflict than your adolescents. In fact, parents tend to report more conflict with their teens than vice versa. This is yet another reason to stay positive; you as a stepparent may be overrating the amount of conflict in the home. Things may actually be better than they seem. In an effort to facilitate positive and mutually supportive relationships between you and your teenage stepchildren, we have many suggestions. This is all in an effort to create cohesive and long-lasting families—keep this in mind when referring to the following list:

- *Observe and you will learn.* In the early stages of the new family, take a spectator role so that you can get to know everyone without developing conflict-ridden relationships. Don't just jump right in and change the rules.
- *Listen and you will be heard.* Discuss the extent of your parenting role with your partner and your stepchildren regarding the parameters of your parenting role. This role should be clearly defined in order to encourage understanding between you, your partner, and your stepchildren.
- *Relax and you will enjoy.* In the face of tension and anxiety, try to remain calm and relaxed. Don't fly off the handle or escalate the family's overall level of stress.
- *Always treat their parents well and in turn you will be well treated.* Honor and respect both of the teens' parents whether or not they are actively involved in the children's lives. Learn to cooperate rather than compete with your stepchildren's biological parents. Don't devalue their biological parents or, above all else, describe how you are far superior to one or both of their parents. Also, treat the children's biological parents well. This is really what they want to see. They want to know that their mom or dad is happy and being treated kindly.
- *Stay involved and you will feel connected.* Be available. Teens need to know that you care. Don't allow yourself to be pushed off to the side.
- *Communicate kindly and you will be appreciated.* Make good communication a priority. This includes talking openly and honestly, not breaking your stepchildren's confidence (unless, of course,

safety is an issue), and using a kind, gentle, and supportive tone when interacting with them.

- Be patient and you will be thanked later. Do not expect gratitude initially. Remember, this is a new and fragile relationship and it will take a while before everyone starts working together.

- Always try to be your best self. Examine and think through what you are trying to accomplish and don't just say whatever it is that you are feeling at the moment without regard for either your own or the teens' feelings and dignity.

- Respect yourself and you will be respected. Take care of yourself while adjusting to the stress of creating a new family: exercise, stay engaged in hobbies, talk to your friends who are involved in similar circumstances, and eat well. Pat yourself on the back even after a particularly difficult day. You have embarked on a challenging journey with a stepfamily and deserve recognition and acknowledgment for all aspects of your confusing new role.

- Cooperate and you will be included. Help the teens with their transition back home when they return from visiting their noncustodial parents. Teens experience stress when returning from visits. It's not easy to move from one set of parents to another.

- Show your commitment. Be aware that your stepchildren may test you to see if you will leave them. Remind them when it's appropriate that you plan to be with them for the long run.

- Praise and you will be consulted. Try to find something positive to value in each of the children in your life. This includes your biological kids and your stepchildren. This will make them each feel valued and will make it more likely that they will get along with each other. They will feel less competitive.

- Remember that you are an adult and you will be called upon for guidance. Do not take the bait when the teenagers try to dump their negative feelings on you. Try to deflect, defuse, and stay calm. This is the best way to give them the message that you will not engage in negativity.

The takeaway message from us here is very positive. The likelihood that you will fare well with your teen stepchildren and even enjoy this role increases with every moment that you practice the skills in the above list. We are handing you the skills and guidelines that you need to open yourself up to communication with your stepchildren. Incorporate them into your everyday interactions and you are likely to find yourself in a role you find not only satisfying but fulfilling. These situations will ensure that you, your partner, and your stepchildren feel good.

Finally, we feel compelled to remind you that as a stepparent you will certainly make some mistakes in your attempts to do the right things. If you feel that you have misstepped, there is always room for recovery and repair work. Please refer to the Second Chance Request info under "Other Nonverbal Cues" in Chapter 3 for ideas about how to recover from situations that have deteriorated.

Joint Custody: Ensuring a Joint Effort

A growing number of divorced parents are making the decision to partner in childcare. On the surface this may seem like the most optimal of situations. However, if you are a parent who has chosen this course, you know firsthand that this path is not without its own bumps in the road. Coparenting is fraught with many challenges and you may be experiencing some difficulties you initially did not consider. The following sections offer some suggestions to ensure a situation that is amicable for all.

Include Your Teens in the Decision

If you have recently made the decision to divorce and are in the process of formulating a joint custody agreement, ask your teens for input. Talk with them about how they envision the agreement to work. It is helpful if you and your ex have this discussion together with your teens. This demonstrates that despite your differences, you and your ex are able to work together on issues that focus on your teens. If you have been divorced for a while, check in with your children periodically to make sure that the initial terms are still working for them.

Design an Arrangement That Works for Everyone

If you have or are in the process of developing a joint custody agreement, we believe that you are truly putting in the greatest of effort to create a situation that allows you and your ex-partner to share in the responsibility and pleasure of raising your children. However, arrangements that are less than optimal for teens are sometimes put in place despite your best intentions. One common concern we have heard from some of the teens we have worked with is how difficult it can be to switch back and forth from home to home.

Consider this: If organization is not your teens' greatest strength, imagine how difficult it must be to keep track of books and other belongings if your agreement involves going from house to house regularly. This arrangement can be overwhelming and frustrating. This is why it is so important to discuss with your teens the type of schedule that works for them. Many of the teens we work with report that it is helpful to have one parent's home serve as the main base. If you and your partner are determined to split time between homes (this is a helpful agreement for working parents who must travel often), devise a schedule which involves one home serving as the base for at least weekly blocks of time. This will help reduce the stress of your teens keeping track of where all their stuff has gone.

GET THEM **TALKING**

"Did the mall have any good sales?"
Even though you generally want to avoid yes/no questions, in this case you can expect an answer and then a segue into how their day at the mall went.

Avoid Arguing over Equitable Time

In an effort to maximize their custody rights some parents get caught up in ensuring that they get just as much time with their teens as their ex-partner. This can result in your teens feeling like the time spent with you has been imposed upon them, which does not bode well for building positive relationships with your teens. It is important to remain flexible and understanding. If your teens are requesting a change one day—or week—listen to their reasoning and make your decision from the standpoint of a concerned parent, not as a competitor in a sparring match with your ex-partner to win the most time with your teens just for the sake of winning.

Don't Get Caught Up in a Split

By now we are sure you understand the importance of consistency between parents, especially when it comes to setting rules and providing consequences. Even with uniformity in place, however, there is still the potential for your teens to appeal to each parent individually in an attempt to get what they want. This type of behavior is not only typical, but in many situations expected. You can prevent your teens from splitting you and your ex by asking direct questions such as "What does your mother/father say about this?" As a follow up, be sure to communicate directly with your ex about any grey areas. Avoid attempts to win your teens over by being the good parent. The more consistency you can provide, the better off your teens will be in the long run; you and your ex-partner will send the message that, despite your differences, you are on the same page as parents. If you do decide to bend the rules in a specific situation, it is in the best interests of everybody to make sure your teens' other parent is aware.

The Role of the Noncustodial Parent

The role of the noncustodial parent is likely the most difficult parental role to negotiate. Although we believe that you should try your hardest to remain involved, we are painfully aware that the storm of emotions kicked off by divorce can interfere with the relationship between you and your teens. Although the role may be challenging, with the right approach, you can keep the relationship with your teens intact.

REPETITIVE LEG OR FOOT SHAKING:

1. A gesture that conveys discomfort.
PARENT: "How was your visit to your dad's house?"

TEENAGER: Shakes legs and feet repetitively.

SUGGESTED PARENTAL RESPONSE: Obviously, this is not the right time to talk. Suggest that your teen talk about this later if he wishes to.

2. A gesture indicating that the conversation is going on too long.
PARENT: "So then, what happened?"

TEENAGER: Begins to vigorously shake legs and feet.

SUGGESTED PARENTAL RESPONSE: Acknowledge that the dialogue needs to be discontinued. Perhaps you can say something like "Maybe we can talk about this at another time." Your goal is to leave the door open for future dialogue.

3. Movements that indicate a sense of restlessness and preoccupation.
PARENT: "It's so nice to see you and your friends."

TEENAGER: Vigorous leg and foot shaking.

SUGGESTED PARENTAL RESPONSE: "It seems like you have lots to do; have fun and stay safe."

Stay Connected Even in the Face of an Angry Teen or Angry Custodial Parent

Although, as the noncustodial parent, it may at times feel as though you would be better served just disappearing, your teens need you. By making the effort to be there and stand by your kids, you send them the message that despite the changes in family life, you are still just as invested in them as you have always been. In fact, visitation may offer an opportunity to forge even more enriching relationships with your teens, especially if prior to the divorce most of the parenting was left to your ex-partner. Your kids will appreciate you for this in the long term.

Allow Your Teens Input Regarding the Visitation Agreement

Some teens sometimes report that they feel that visitation with their noncustodial parent has been imposed on them. As if their lives had not been turned upside down enough, they don't have input about when and how often they can spend time with you. As highlighted above, if you allow your teens to have some say regarding visitation, you send them the message that what they have to say matters. If their proposals are unrealistic or unacceptable to either you or your ex-partner, take the time to talk it out with them.

Do Not Give Up

On occasion, when a family split has occurred, family members take sides. If you feel that your teens have chosen their other parent over you, it is important to stay involved now more than ever. If they seem less than pleased to talk with or see you, roll with it. While we recommend persistence, do not hover. Instead, look for opportunities to interact. If their response to you is negative, give them space but continue to check in with them. When the opportunity arises, let them know directly that you care about them and are not going to give up. If your past behavior (toward them or their other parent) is not something you are proud of, have an honest conversation about this, and acknowledge your mistakes and regrets. An apology can go a long way. Give your teens the time and space they need, but do not check out. You will want to be there when they finally come around.

Stay Away from any Negative Discussion of the Custodial Parent or Stepparents

Although your teens may want to vent about their custodial or stepparents, they certainly don't benefit from having you join in. You should also be wary of taking all the content of these rants as gospel. Remember, these are their points of view. Your teens are using this time with you to express their feelings; they are confiding in you. The last thing they need is for you to take their words and confront their custodial parent with them. If your teens do report something about which you are concerned, talk with them further; get the facts. Only then should you talk with their custodial parent. We can assure you that the majority of the time your teens are just blowing off steam. You should be happy that they feel close enough with you to relieve this type of stress in your presence.

Help Your Teens with the Transition from Your Home to Their Custodial Parent's Home.

Everyone, including teens, experiences some degree of stress when going from one type of situation to another. Whenever possible, be present to greet your teens when they arrive at your home. If you are working and they will get to your house before you will, leave them a note to greet them and/or require a check-in call as soon as they arrive. This will send the message that you are not only aware that it is your turn to spend time with them, but that you are excited about it. When your teens come to visit, make sure you have set up a designated space for them to sleep, do school work, and hang out. They should feel like your home is also their home. You do not want them to feel like a guest as this can lead to distance and awkward moments.

Work with Their Custodial Parent to Present a Unified Front

Rules between houses should be consistent. This will save everybody—especially your teens—a lot of stress and ensure that your teens will not try to play parent against parent. Work with your teens to create any rules that may be specific to your home due to unique situations or circumstances that may differ between your home and their custodial parent's home. Keep the custodial parent informed about these additions.

Understand That Most Teens Spend More Time with Their Peers Than with Their Parents

Try to honor this and not take it personally. If you and the custodial parent do not live close to one another and your teens request some changes to the visitation agreement due to upcoming events with their friends, hear them out and be reasonable. Do not insist that every second lost with you needs to be renegotiated with their custodial parent. You want your teens to look forward to their time with you. You do not want them to view visitation as a chore or a burden. If their requests to change the schedule become unreasonable, talk to them about this. Let them know that you value your time with them. Try to work out a plan that pleases all of you.

GET THEM TALKING

"I bet your mom/dad was really happy to see you."
A kind comment about the noncustodial parent may lead to a discussion of how their weekend went.

Be Patient

Allow some time for everyone involved to get comfortable with the new schedule. Change is hard and it is even harder when it is brought on by difficult or emotionally charged circumstances. Even if the break with the custodial parent is quite amicable, your teens may not see it that way. They may need time to process all their mixed emotions. Provide opportunities for them to talk about the changes. If they are less than willing, do not push them. As we have pointed our already, sometimes it is what you don't say that can make all the difference. Give them space and time to settle down. With a lot of support and understanding your teens will settle in to the new routine.

Try to Involve Your Teens in Your New Family with Grace, Dignity, and Patience for All Involved

We discussed the difficulties involved with stepparenting earlier in this chapter, but blending families when you are the noncustodial parent offers a whole separate set of challenges and necessitates being mindful of everyone's feelings. While it would be great if you could just say "Okay, everybody let's just get along," and they did, unfortunately, the blending of families takes time and tolerance. Because your teens do not spend the majority of their time with you, you and your new family have most likely developed a rhythm and routine to your daily lives that your teens are not familiar with. When your teens come to visit however, they may not only disrupt the routine, but refuse to participate. Keep in mind that, from a developmental standpoint, adolescents are egocentric (see Chapter 1) and the mere fact that you have a new family can be a difficult and sometimes painful idea for them to manage. You go on with your life when they are not there. They may feel as if the new family members are living the life that once belonged to them.

It is important to acknowledge the changes that have taken place. Sometimes parents, in an effort to move the blending of a family along, go about business as usual when their teens come to visit. From your teens' perspectives, however, this is not so. Their lives have been changed and the last thing they want to see is that you have simply moved on as if their family life with you and the custodial parent never existed. Encourage stepparents to read through the tips we have offered in previous sections. Continue to involve you teens in your new family and in time they will feel part of it. In addition, if you have recently had a new baby or are expecting, include your teens fully in this exciting event. Often the miracle of the birth of a new baby can be a great mediator. By including your teens in the process you truly highlight the importance of blending the old with the new.

Again, it is vital that you make every attempt to keep the lines of communication open regarding these changes. You do not want your teens to walk away feeling like they are no longer important parts of your life, that they have been replaced, or that they no longer matter. If your teens seem withdrawn or, in extreme situations, hostile toward your new family, find time to address this with them. Also, make sure to set aside time to spend just with them, without the rest of the new family. Your response to them can make all the difference.

Make Your Teens a Priority

Although your kids may be older, they need you now more than ever. Whether your role as a noncustodial parent is new or a hat you have worn for quite a while now, your role as a parent should remain consistent. While it may be easy to convince yourself that out of sight really is out of mind we can assure you that your teens probably do not see it this way. The teen years are your children's gateway to adulthood and it is important that you are there to provide support and guidance. We understand that life gets in the way and we understand that, at a time when your kids are focused on spending so much time with their friends, it may seem like they do not need you, but let us assure you, this couldn't be further from the truth.

While your teens may not seem as accessible to you, perhaps they are changing or canceling visitation days due to their busy lives, it is important that you do not respond in kind. You need to send them the message that you are easily accessible and available. Now we are not suggesting that if they change days or break plans with you that you sit around waiting for them. We are simply stating that it is important that you understand that this behavior does not mean they no longer need you or want to be with you. Invest the time and continue to build a relationship with your teens. The benefits are great and satisfying!

No matter what role you play in the family—breadwinner, primary caretaker, custodial or noncustodial parent, stepparent—your role as a parent is extremely important. Your communication style should always reflect a positive attitude, love, and patience.

As families evolve, parents need a new set of guiding principles. We have described various types of family configurations. Below we offer a set of strategies.

1. **Roles May Have Changed but the Job Description Remains the Same:** No matter how the role of the parent may have evolved over the last few decades, the responsibilities and expectations of the job remain the same.

2. **All Work and No Play Is Never a Good Idea:** Working from home has many benefits. By creating a set of structured rules and boundaries regarding your work, you will not get stuck in the trap of making home a twenty-four-hour office. Communicate clearly with your teens about if and when you are available and you are sure to be not only productive at your work but more available to your family.

3. **You Can Have It All:** The competing demands of being a full-time parent and breadwinner may at times feel overwhelming. By implementing a check-in system with your teens and planning ahead to arrange rides, making connections within your community, and ensuring attendance at your teens' games and performances, you can master this delicate juggling act.

4. **Careful Steps Get You Where You Want to Go Faster:** By treading patiently and thoughtfully stepparents can build

wonderful relationships with their stepchildren. Clearly defining the role of the stepparent is the key to peace and harmony in your home.

5. **Focus on Your Teens Not on the Agreement:** If you get caught up in a battle over enforcing the rules of a custody agreement, you may lose sight of the purpose of such an agreement, to continue to be an integral part of your teens' lives. By maintaining a flexible approach to these formal agreements, you send the message to your teens that you understand how busy their lives can get and want to support them.

6. **Communication Is Always the Key to Success:** Regardless of your role or title, the way to ensure a happy and healthy home is to make sure that you talk to each other. When you communicate well with your partner, ex, or teens' stepparents you model how to maintain positive interactions. When you listen and hear your teens you demonstrate how a little talking goes a long way.

CHAPTER 7

Everything but the Kitchen Sink: Talking with Your Teen about Sensitive Topics

In life we are often faced with the unexpected, including events and topics that are particularly difficult to talk about. Although starting these conversations is not easy, they must be started and taken to conclusion. We believe that it is important to begin talking with your children about important or difficult topics when they are very young; this history of honest dialogue will make it easier for you to talk about sensitive topics with them as they become teens. Although there are countless sensitive topics, in this chapter we limit our advice to a smattering of a few. Our hope is that you can follow the model we provide when addressing any additional sensitive topics that come your way.

When Your Teen Has a Chronic Illness

If your teen is managing a chronic illness it may bring you and him some solace to know that he is not alone. A chronic condition is defined as any problem that lasts at least twelve months and results in physical limitations, requires consistent monitoring or mediation (through apparatus and/or medication), or additional services (such as educational or physical therapy). It has been estimated that close to 15 percent of teens manage some sort of chronic illness. Chronic conditions include but are not limited to:

- Diabetes.
- Asthma.
- Genetic disorders (such as Marfan syndrome).
- Skin conditions (such as psoriasis or eczema).
- Cystic fibrosis.
- Cancer.
- Sickle cell disease.
- Rheumatoid arthritis.
- Congenital heart disease.
- Cerebral palsy.
- Epilepsy.
- Attention-deficit/hyperactivity disorder.
- Mood disorders (such as bipolar disorder or depression).
- Anxiety disorders.

Managing a chronic illness can result in additional stress for the entire family. In addition to parents and the affected teens, siblings are prone to feel an impact as well.

What Chronically Ill Teens Have to Say

Most affected teens rely on their parents to manage their illnesses and direct treatment regimes. One concern some of these teens voice, however, is that they sometimes feel that they are not included enough in the information about and decisions regarding their own illnesses. Many teens indicate that they want more direct access to the information provided by the healthcare professionals involved in their treatment. Parents acknowledge their role as the gatekeepers and some report that they purposely withhold important information from their teens regarding the illnesses in an effort to protect them. While your teens may appreciate your role as information managers, they report that it is important for you and healthcare providers to realize that the illnesses are happening to them and they want to be kept more in the loop. They want to be talked *with,* not at.

SAD SMILES (SMILES THAT INVOLVE THE LIPS ONLY, WITHOUT ANY MOVEMENT OF THE MUSCLES AROUND THE EYES):

1. An expression that is an attempt to fake happiness.
PARENT: "Are you happy about that?"
TEENAGER: Sad smile.
SUGGESTED PARENTAL RESPONSE: Acknowledge that she may be less than happy by saying something like "You don't look too pleased."

2. An attempt to convey that this is not the right moment to talk about things.
PARENT: "Was the sleepover fun?"
TEENAGER: Sad smile.
SUGGESTED PARENTAL RESPONSE: In an attempt to be in tune with her, perhaps you can say "We can talk about it later if you like."

Because of their conditions, your chronically ill teens may be more dependent on you than their healthy peers. This is especially true at times when their illnesses flare up or cause complications in their ability to manage the responsibilities of daily living such as attending school or participating in extracurricular activities. While illness can lead to social isolation and an increased risk of anxiety and depression, a highly supportive family can mediate and diminish these effects. However, it's important to know that your affected teens may feel that you and their siblings are more attentive (and in some cases more controlling) when their illnesses' symptoms are present. As a result, your teens may actually feign symptoms or severity of symptoms to reap personal benefits such as getting out of chores or tasks they do not want to perform, missing school, and/or receiving extra attention from parents or siblings. When your affected teens perceive that you are closely monitoring their illness and treatment protocols, they are more likely to follow through with prescribed treatment regimes and symptom-management recommendations.

It's important for your teens to accept and be open about their illnesses. They put themselves at risk when they try to keep their situations a secret from peers and teachers. Most affected teens miss many days of school and this is often reflected in poor academic performance in comparison to their healthy peers, especially because their absence patterns tend to be sporadic. Missing a day here and there can lead to inconsistency and without effective mediation teens can become overwhelmed and stressed at school. Because your teens want to be like everyone else they may take unnecessary risks in an effort to keep up with their peers, but they are likely to fare better if they acknowledge their limitations.

Your teens may be noncompliant with treatment if they experience side effects or are thwarted from activities. Teens afflicted with type 1 diabetes, for example, may resent the diet restrictions by which they must abide and therefore disregard or cheat. The severity of their illness will dictate the impact. This type of rebellion, although potentially dangerous, is consistent with adolescent development (see Chapters 1 and 4). Interestingly, as your teens get older their compliance with treatment regimes have been noted to decrease. This may be due in part to their desire to affirm their own independence as well as their developmental belief (as noted in Chapter 1) that they are invulnerable. Your chronically ill teens' frustrations related to the limitations enforced by their illnesses can put them at higher risk than healthy teens to use drugs and alcohol or to engage in sexual activities as a way to cope with these feelings and to feel they fit in with their peers.

How Parents Should Respond: Transitioning Chronically Ill Teens to Self-Management

Coming of age includes a host of tasks and challenges for the average teen, but the challenges are even greater for ones dealing with chronic illnesses. As outlined in Chapter 4, the road to autonomy and independence is marked by teens' increasing awareness about the world around them, and for chronically ill teens, adolescence should include making the transition from you managing their illnesses to self-management. A successful transition relies on groundwork laid throughout childhood and adolescence. As with other adolescent accomplishments, there is no magic age that determines when a teen is ready to assume this responsibility. Instead, readiness should be decided on an individual basis. We offer the following guidelines to you on how to encourage a successful transition:

1. *The transition to self-management should take place over time.* You should work with your teens to gradually increase their self-care responsibilities. It is important that your teens have a full understanding of their conditions. It is your role to gauge your teens' cognitive ability to understand the information provided. You can do this by talking with them directly. Create opportunities to discuss their symptoms and treatment protocols and keep up on the latest information available and share the information with them.

2. *Once you have determined that your teens are cognitively ready to take on more responsibility for self-management allow them to do so.* Do not let your own anxiety get in the way of encouraging this process. Teens are more likely to appropriately assume responsibility for their illnesses when parents relinquish control. If you say you are not in control, but continue to act in a controlling manner, you run the risk of your teens rebelling in unhealthy, noncompliant ways.

3. *Establish a transition plan with your teens that encourages self-monitoring but allows you to ensure that your teens are compliant.* Establishing appropriate guidelines for your teens' care by working with them closely will make everyone feel comfortable and will also avoid conflict. If your teens know you will be involved in overseeing their compliance and adherence, they

will not feel as if you are trying to control the process. This approach also encourages your teens to use you as a resource instead of cutting you out of the loop.

4. *Involve healthcare providers in the transition plan.* During scheduled appointments, encourage your teens to meet with their healthcare providers alone first. You should join them for a recap to ensure that you each understand any recommendations or changes in treatment protocol.

In addition to the previous suggestions, you should also encourage your teens to establish an outside support network. The road toward independence is paved with support from the sidelines. While most teens strive to establish their own independence, they thrive on acceptance and understanding from those around them. Chronically ill teens must face the additional struggle of integrating their illnesses into their identities. Your teens may believe that no one understands them and that no one else could possibly think, feel, and experience what they have—especially you. This is in part why your chronically ill teens are more vulnerable to depression and anxiety than healthy teens. Support groups provide teens with protective factors; your teens can even attend groups or connect directly with other affected teens via the Internet. This type of support can be invaluable because it provides instant access to others who actually understand and get it. This type of support is invaluable as your teens move toward managing their illnesses on their own.

Remember, your chronically ill teens will face more challenges than their healthy peers. The type and severity of illnesses your teens are managing will in many cases dictate the lifestyle adjustments necessary to ensure health. You can help normalize your teens' experiences by following the guidelines we have suggested.

Financial Difficulties and/or Job Loss

As you have probably already realized, your teens are like sponges. They quickly soak up information. As we discussed in Chapter 1, your teens possess a newfound awareness of the world around them. If your family is experiencing financial stress, it is likely that your teens are aware that something is going on. Sometimes this awareness is linked more to the subtle shifts in your mood and attitude. It is not uncommon during economic distress, for example, for parents to come across as less nurturing and more punitive. In addition, during such times, your discipline may become less consistent and your monitoring of your teens' activities less frequent. These shifts in mood and behavior, in turn, affect your teens who may feel less self-assured and more in distress.

This type of stress affects girls and boys differently. Several studies have even demonstrated that your daughters are especially prone to decreases in self-esteem and may become less hopeful about their own future professional successes in the face of your financial woes. In turn, these declines may be reflected in feelings of social and or academic incompetence. In contrast, your sons may become more reliant on their peers for support and guidance. It seems that, in general, your sons' own professional ambitions will not usually be affected by your family's financial distress, but if they are, it is actually in a positive way in that teen boys may be more driven to succeed. This probably results because they push themselves to learn from the situation that their families find themselves in. However due to these family difficulties, your sons may appear more distant from you and may engage in delinquent behaviors and drug use during periods of economic stress. Both your daughters and sons may experience depression and loneliness in response to family economic hardship.

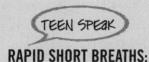

RAPID SHORT BREATHS:

1. A behavior that may indicate high anxiety.
PARENT: "I want you to finish your applications tonight."

TEENAGER: Rapid short breaths.

SUGGESTED PARENTAL RESPONSE: Since your teen is likely anxious, say something soothing like "Maybe doing them all in one night is a lot."

2. A symptom of respiratory illness.
PARENT: "This is a nice conversation."

TEENAGER: Rapid short breaths.

SUGGESTED PARENTAL RESPONSE: Ask your teen if he is feeling well. Sometimes he will need to be encouraged to tell you that he is not feeling well physically.

Your teens may also deal with these types of stress by distancing themselves from the family or by experiencing denial. This response may concern and frustrate you. If, for example, your teenagers suddenly begin to demand more from you such as the newest hi-tech gadgets or expensive shoes, this may be their way of managing. Because your teens feel that they can't control the situation, denial is another way for them to manage the related stress. Your teens may approach the situation by trying to take some control. They may, for example, decide to get jobs with the intent of lessening the burden by earning their own spending money. In extreme cases of financial stress they may offer their earnings to help support the family.

If your teens are facing a major transition during the time of economic stress, such as transitioning from middle school to high school, the stress they may be experiencing can be compounded. A 1993 study shows that this sometimes translates into a decline in academic achievement and/or acting out or withdrawal behaviors in the classroom. If the financial situation requires major lifestyle changes such as moving and or switching schools your teens can experience depression and loneliness. Adolescence is usually a time when individuals are highly reliant on their peer groups for support and it is not uncommon for your teens to feel embarrassed or ashamed about their families' financial situations. This can result in distancing themselves or even withdrawing from peers.

GET THEM TALKING

"Come outside and look at my garden."
You are demonstrating availability and interest. Teens are more likely to talk to you if you are around and not busy with another task.

How You Should Respond

Financial stress affects the whole family. We hope that by enlightening you about what your teens may be experiencing you can lessen the impact by responding in ways which reduce the stress and concern your teens may be experiencing. We acknowledge that when you are managing your own anxieties this can be difficult and this is why a discussion about the family finances between you and your teens must include an overview and acknowledgment of how the situation is affecting you and/or your partner. The difficulty lies in striking the balance between offering enough information to promote understanding and reassurance in your teens and providing too many details which can result in your teens feeling overwhelmed, anxious, and depressed. We offer the following list as guidelines for coping.

1. *In a calm and caring manner invite your teens to talk with you.* Start by gently presenting the situation. For example say something like, "As you probably know things have gotten a little more difficult because . . . ." Assume they know something (which they probably do). Even if they don't, this will make them feel empowered. The message you send them with this approach is that you believe they are in tune with what is going on in the family. Provide only information that is necessary. If, for example, you or your partner has lost a job state the facts, but spare the details.

2. *Offer a brief overview of the immediate impact of the situation and focus on how or if it will affect your teens.* By offering your teens these insights you create predictability and structure. This may help to quell some of the anxiety they may experience regarding the changes. For example, you may want to say something like, "We are going to be okay. It may just mean that we all have to find ways to cut back a little. Let's talk about how that may affect you . . . ."

3. *Offer a brief overview of the impact the situation may have on the future.* For example, you could say something like, "We are hopeful that things will pick up soon but if not, this is how you might be affected in the future . . . ." Again focus on how or if it will affect your teens; don't just say, "If things don't get better soon you are going to have to make big changes" and then leave it at that.

4. *Outline your intended plan of action including a timeline if possible.* Avoid a detailed step-by-step analysis. This will provide your teens with the sense that although the situation is difficult it is under control, which should help reduce some of the anxiety your teens may be experiencing. Focus on the positive. If, for example, the situation will require the family to sell the house, emphasize the excitement of finding a new place to live and or moving in with relatives. Say something like, "I know it will be difficult to move but let's check out the listings together to find our new place" or "Grandma is so excited that we are moving in with her. I know it will be difficult to move but at least we have each other."

5. *Invite your teens to ask questions.* Be sure to treat these questions seriously and answer in as reassuring a manner as possible.

6. *End the discussion when it is clear that your teens are ready.* Your teens will offer you verbal and nonverbal cues that the discussion should end. Pay attention so that you recognize and acknowledge these cues.

7. *Reassure your teens that you will keep them updated on the situation.* Be careful to avoid constant updates, which may include too much detail. For example, if you are having difficulty paying your mortgage one month, work out a plan with your lender, but

do not provide this information to your teens. However, if your teens pick up on the situation and ask you how you are planning to pay the mortgage you should reassure them that you are working out a plan. You may want to say something like, "Feel free to ask any questions or discuss any concerns with me as they come up. I love you and we will get through this."

8. *Do not put your teens in the role of consultant or confidante about the situation.* This could result in your teens feeling overwhelmed, anxious, and depressed. If you are a single parent it is important to establish a support network for yourself. This will prevent you from unintentionally relying on your teens to provide this type of advice and understanding.

9. *End the discussion by assuring your teens that you are available to answer any questions or to discuss the situation.* Most importantly, conclude the conversation on a positive note. This will send the message that no matter what things will be okay.

Teens in Military Families

How teens adjust to having parents in the military is a topic that is often overlooked. However, more and more parents are deployed on multiple occasions and for longer periods of time making this a topic that we believe deserves acknowledgment. If you are a military family, your teens face multiple stressors. In addition to the task of being a teen who is trying to separate and gain autonomy from you (see Chapter 4), your teen needs to do this in the context of being a member of a military family. As you may already realize, the frequent moves and long periods of separation can cause much stress. And, in fact, adolescents in military families face three critical time periods that are uniquely stressful to their situations. These include the initial period of separating and deployment, the separation period itself, and the reunion. We address all three of these major periods of adjustment separately as they are all associated with their own unique set of stressors.

SLOUCHING OR MARKED DROOPING OF SHOULDERS (PARTICULARLY OBVIOUS WHEN YOUR TEENAGER IS SITTING):

1. Suggests unhappiness and stress.

PARENT: "Are you okay?"

TEENAGER: "I'm fine." (While sinking deeper into the couch; tone of voice suggests teenager does not want to discuss further.)

SUGGESTED PARENTAL RESPONSE: "I'm here if you want to talk." You should then walk away unless the teen responds. At this point in time the teen is most likely feeling something that he is not eager to discuss and would very likely appreciate some space. By all means try to respect this.

2. Lost in thought but feeling fine.

PARENT: "Are you okay?"

TEENAGER: "I'm fine." (Tone of voice suggests distance as when one responds when daydreaming.)

SUGGESTED PARENTAL RESPONSE: Again, let your teenager know that you are available to talk at another time.

Preparing for a Parent's Departure and Deployment

Your teens have a greater understanding than their younger siblings of the dangers associated with deployment to a war zone and its association with death and injury. They are, therefore, more likely to be impacted than their younger siblings. A 2007 study published in *Military Medicine* found that these adolescents are more vulnerable to physiological symptoms of anxiety including higher blood pressure and increased heart rates in comparison to peers who are not from military families.

Teens may also have more exposure to media than their younger siblings and this, too, may increase their fears about your safety. They are more likely to have knowledge about controversies surrounding particular wars and may be frightened and confused by any antiwar sentiments especially put forth by the media. You may believe that due to their age, your teens are less in need of discussion and emotional preparation than your younger children. Hence, you may be unintentionally ignoring your teens' needs. Remember, your teens need you even though they often push you away. In fact, in the confused language of *Teenage*, your teens may push you away, at a time when they need you most.

When Your Teens Are Having Difficulty Dealing with a Parent's Departure

Your teens may try to communicate their difficulty managing your or your partner's departure both verbally and nonverbally. Their communication may be manifested in many aspects of their behavior including:

1. Lingering around you.
2. Avoiding usual activities.

3. An increase in somatic symptoms (physical symptoms are also a form of language).

4. Sleep disturbance.

5. Clinginess. (Teens cling when they are afraid of loss. This is not necessarily specific to teens, however. Consider your own push–pull behavior when you are scared of losing someone.)

6. Hypervigilance. (This refers to frequent attempts to gather information by being overly attentive to the environment. This includes what is being said as well as to how others are behaving and feeling.)

7. Overly cheerful behavior. (This may indicate an attempt to mask genuine and scary feelings.)

8. Greater demands for attention.

9. Decreasing academic performance.

10. Acting-out behaviors. (This is more frequently the language of adolescent boys who may deal with emotions by engaging in behaviors such as substance use, physical aggression, and other externalizing behaviors.)

11. Isolative behavior.

12. Avoidant behavior.

What you may notice in the list above is that some of the behaviors appear to be the direct opposites of others. This can be the result of the mix of feelings that your teens are experiencing regarding the impending deployment. We refer to this as the language of push–pull behavior. Teens alternate attempts to engage with you and attempts to push you away. Remember, it is difficult enough to do the work of normal adolescent separation. Imagine trying to separate in the context of having a parent going off to war and possibly facing injury or even death.

You can help your teens cope during a parent's deployment by following the guidelines we have put forth. Additionally, use the following techniques to make the upcoming departure a little easier.

TRY THIS	RATHER THAN THIS
Speak to your teens about their feelings about the separation.	Avoid all discussion. After all, why stir up emotions?
Provide some limits to media images of war as this can be overwhelmingly scary to teens.	Let them watch war coverage constantly. You are scared so they might as well share your fears.
Let your teens know that you are always available to talk to them about their sadness and anxiety.	Only talk to them when they have something positive to say. You already have enough stress without having to deal with theirs.
Talk to your teens and arrange, if possible, how they can stay connected to the deployed parent while they are away. Set up a system of contact, which may include mail, care packages, and phone, and/or e-mail contact.	Let them figure this out on their own. They need to be tough, get on with life, and make their own arrangements to make contact.
Work on your own positive outlook and attitude. Remember, you are powerful role models for your teens.	Be as negative and pessimistic as you want. This is your life too.

Handling the Period of Separation

Your teens face many of the same problems and reactions during this period as they do when parents initially leave for the military. However, there is an additional set of difficulties. A 2008 overview published in *Youth & Society* found that adolescent depression, irritability, impulsiveness, and emotional health in general are related to parental deployment. Your teens may have a harder time dealing with the separation if the deployed parent is in a combat situation and/or if their tour of duty is particularly long. Your teens' reactions tend, not surprisingly, to reflect the reactions of the parent who is at home with them. In order to facilitate the well-being of your teens during the period of separation we recommend you try the suggestions in the following table.

TRY THIS	RATHER THAN THIS
Try not to overburden your teens with parental responsibilities as they already are likely to have busy schedules.	Have your teens do all of the household chores and take care of the younger children.
Seek out support and help for your own feelings of loneliness, anxiety, and depression. When you adapt well to the period of separation, your teens are likely to follow suit.	Ignore your own feelings. Your teens don't pay attention to you anyway.
Allow your teens to go to their usual activities and develop a predictable family schedule.	You have so much on your mind that you might as well let the teens do whatever makes them happy. Routines and schedules can wait until their absent parent rejoins the family.

Adjusting to the Reunion as a Parent Returns from Deployment

Surprisingly, a parent's return home may be as or more stressful than the period of deployment itself. During the period of deployment, your family may develop new routines, shift roles and responsibilities, and begin to feel distant from the deployed parent. Adolescents report difficulty with the shift in roles especially when it is their father who has been deployed as fathers attempt to reassume their predeployment roles and responsibilities. If household routines change, teens experience further stress. Your teens may also sometimes report feeling that they need to spend all of their free time with the returning parent perhaps in order to get reacquainted or simply to make up for lost time. You can imagine how this might lead to resentment and anxiety. This transition can impact your teens even more if their parent comes back changed either or both emotionally and physically.

We are not suggesting that there are only negative aspects of a parent's return home. Of course, this is generally a happy occurrence. Nonetheless, this reunion period is fraught with stress. In the following table we provide some guidelines for you to make the reunion period go more smoothly.

TRY THIS	RATHER THAN THIS
Try not to rush into changing roles and responsibilities too quickly. Pace yourselves and make changes gradually. Everyone needs time to readjust.	Change everything quickly. Why waste time?
Allow your teens to spend their free time in a variety of ways. Try not to make them feel a sense of urgency about getting reacquainted with the returning parent.	Demand that they spend all of their free time with the returning parent.
As in all situations, encourage your teens to talk about their feelings and the difficulties and excitement about the reunion. Try not to either over- or under-react to what they have to say.	Do not provide opportunities for the expression of feelings. You, as parents, are having enough of your own problems.

Just as teens within military families deal with mixed and confusing feelings, teens who are being bullied experience a similar set of feelings. Different sets of circumstances may lead to similar difficulties.

Helping Your Teens Deal with Bullying

As we are all aware, being bullied—whether physically, verbally, or emotionally—can be a devastating experience. Bullying is consistently delivered with the intent of one person trying to hurt another weaker person and often includes physical attacks, teasing, starting rumors, name-calling, and excluding others from social groups and interactions, all of which result in negative emotional effects such as sadness, anxiety, and low self-esteem. Bullies tend to engage in their behavior repeatedly and their behavior is ordinarily not limited to a single incident. Although bullying frequently occurs outside of the home, particularly in the school setting, it is now entering the victims' homes in the form of cyberbullying. If your teens are bullied outside of the home they may now feel unsafe within the home if they have received bullying threats via text messages and/or the Internet.

GET THEM TALKING

"You make me laugh. You're a great storyteller."

Teens who are praised are more likely to talk to you.

Your teens, like children of all ages, are especially likely to keep their experiences of being bullied to themselves because they probably feel deeply ashamed, feeling helpless, and are afraid of upsetting and/or disappointing you. They may, nonetheless, relate their struggles to you nonverbally. If you notice a cluster of nonverbal signs, your teens may be telling you they are being teased. These signs include:

1. Sadness.
2. Social withdrawal and isolation.
3. Anxiety.
4. Physical complaints or injuries.
5. Attempting to avoid school or refusal to attend school.
6. Deteriorating academic performance.
7. Difficulty concentrating.
8. Destroyed property.
9. Missing items.
10. Taking a new path to school.
11. Being reluctant to take the school bus.
12. Taking your money.

What all of these behaviors have in common is that your teens are behaving somewhat differently than usual. There is a shift in their nonverbal communication in a negative direction. If your teens are being bullied they may try to avoid school, their usual route to school, and the school bus because these are common places where bullying tends to occur. Anxiety, physical complaints, deteriorating grades, sadness, isolation, and focusing problems are clearly tied to being trapped in a world characterized by being a target of meanness and cruelty. Physical injuries and destroyed property may be a result of the behavior of bullies who favor a hands-on approach. If your teens are missing money and stealing from you, they may be embarrassed to tell you that bullies are stealing their money. Hence, they may steal your money to be able to purchase lunch or even in response to threats about what bullies would do to them if they didn't bring money. In either case, money is likely being extorted from them. One note of caution: As discussed in Chapter 2, sometimes teens may also steal money because they are using drugs so it is imperative to sort out the situation before jumping to firm conclusions.

GOOD:

1. An adjective that has the unusual ability to convey feelings from merely good to quite fabulous. One should be cautioned that a flat delivery does not necessarily convey a lack of intensity of feeling or a failed result.

PARENT: "How was the test?"

TEENAGER: "Good."

SUGGESTED PARENTAL RESPONSE: This is an opportunity to respond in a kind and reinforcing manner. The only caution here is not to get overexcited which may be interpreted as pressure.

The previous table focuses on communication styles to be used when your teens are being bullied. For specific skills and strategies for your teen to use to deal with bullying we suggest turning to school personnel and/or professionals.

As a parent, you need to know the signals that your teens are using to communicate that they are being bullied and you need to learn how to respond to their communication. In general it is important that your responses be consistently supportive, respectful, and loving. Your teens are already feeling worthless and vulnerable. They are afraid that you may agree with their bullies' impressions of them. We suggest that you try to figure out if your teens want your help or if they simply want you to listen and absorb some of their feelings. In the following table we give you some ideas of how to most effectively support your teens if they are communicating that they are victims of bullying. In all cases, remember that you should respond from the perspective of a helpful parent rather than from the perspective of an enraged peer. Teens want parents to be parents, not friends.

TRY THIS	RATHER THAN THIS
Listen supportively when your teens make it clear that they just want to talk.	Offer advice.
Stay calm. Neither under- or overreact emotionally.	Become flustered, enraged, and emotionally overwhelmed. Offer to go to school and tell off the bully yourself.
Try to remind your teens about their positive qualities. Everyone likes to be supported when they are feeling down.	Tell your teens that the bullies are right and that your teens are way too sensitive. Perhaps you might even suggest that they should take advice from the bullies.
If your teens are clearly asking for advice then attempt to problem solve with them. When problem solving, keep in mind your teens' strengths and weaknesses. You do not want to make the mistake of suggesting that your teens do something that they do not feel capable of.	Tell your teens to simply ignore and/or stand up to the bullies. This is sure to make them feel even more incompetent.
Get all of the information about where, when, and how frequently the bullying is happening. This will help you and your teens identify patterns. It will also communicate that you are supportive and interested in helping.	Be dismissive. Tune out. Even if your teens want help, communicate disinterest.

TRY THIS	RATHER THAN THIS
Communicate to your teens honestly about whether or not you are going to report these incidents to school personnel or to the authorities. Collaborate with your teens about who the best people at school are for you to talk to.	Talk to school personnel and/or the authorities and leave your teens in the dark about this. This will further support the message from the bullies that your teens are not worthy of respect.
Communicate that there is hope and that either you and your teens or a professional and your teens can work on strategies to reduce bullying. Providing hope and opportunities for learning communicates your belief that your teens have the capacity to learn.	Back off. Tell your teens that they are on their own. Remind them that you never knew what to do when you were being bullied; how can you possibly be expected to help them?
Always communicate your love for your teens by simply listening, giving a pat on the back, giving your child time, and/or simply saying "I love you."	Withhold your love. Express it only when your teens have successfully achieved something worthy of your love.

LET'S REVIEW: TIPS FOR TRANSLATING

In sum we have included just a few of the many unique and sensitive topics you may need to address with your teens during their adolescence. We conclude this chapter by offering you our general model of when and how to talk to your teens about these and other sensitive topics. We leave you with the following guiding principles.

1. **Inform, Don't Insult!:** Ask your teens what they already know. If you make the assumption that they know nothing, you run the risk of them shutting down before the conversation has even started. Correct misperceptions and pace the amount of information you share.

2. **See It from Their Points of View:** Focus on how certain situations will affect your teens' lives. If warranted provide a prospective timeline for resolution.

3. **Remain Responsive, Not Reactive:** Respond to your teens' reactions in a reassuring manner. Keep your own emotional reactions under good control. You do not want to overwhelm your teens.

4. **Acceptance Equals Affirmation:** Reassure your teens that their reactions will be neither judged nor shared with others. By reinforcing honest and sincere dialogue you demonstrate that you are trustworthy and reliable.

5. **Check in During and After:** During a conversation about a sensitive topic check in with your teens to ensure that they are managing and are not on information-overload. Check in with them at some point after a conversation to see if they would like opportunities to get more information.

6. **Seek Advice and Support from the Outside, Not Inside:** Do not rely on your teens to act as a confidante regarding the situation. This can lead to your teen experiencing increased stress, anxiety, and depression.

7. **Support, Support, and Support Some More!:** Family support has been found to be one of the greatest buffers of stress regardless of the situation at hand. Offer that support to your teens.

8. **Focus on the Positive:** No matter how difficult the situation is if you remain calm and positive, your teens are more likely to feel the same way.

Afterword

Congratulations! You now know how to speak *Teenage!* But now that you have become fluent, your goal is to maintain fluency. Remember, when you can talk to your teens in their own language your communication will be easier, your lives will be less fraught with struggles, and your energy will be conserved. You and your teens, having learned to understand each other more easily, will have richer relationships, which are characterized by fewer misunderstandings.

In reviewing the journey that led to your fluency, there are many points to keep in mind.

1. Your teens do want to talk to you, but they want to have some control over the style and timing of the interactions. Always remember this when they are abrupt or silent.
2. Consider their responses as a complicated mixture of verbal and nonverbal language.
3. You will frequently need to rely on intuition but will need to be wary of the effects of the *ESP Factor* which can result in misinterpretation and miscommunication.
4. Sometimes the verbal and nonverbal signals your teens send will be in sync and will provide you with a very clear message. At other times, they may seem to be delivering divergent messages. Our hope is that your new command of *Teenage* will help you successfully sort out the intended meaning of the message.

Always keep in mind that your teens want your support and approval and are hard-pressed to request this, given their need to forge ahead as self-reliant young men and women. Remember this whenever they attempt to confide in you, particularly when the information is potentially sensitive or embarrassing. Respect should characterize the communication styles of all members of the family. It is within a climate of mutual respect that your teenagers will be most likely to speak to you. A positive and supportive family atmosphere results in honest dialogue.

We have the greatest respect for your roles as the parents of teens and we have full confidence in your ability to carefully manage whatever your teens communicate to you. We wish you and your teens smooth talking. Remember, practice makes progress.

RESOURCE LIST

Allard, Mary Dorinda, and Marianne Janes, U.S. Department of Labor, U.S. Bureau of Labor Statistics. "Time Use of Working Parents: A Visual Essay." *Monthly Labor Review*, 131 no. 6 (2008): 3–14.

Arnenson, Karen W. "Applications to Colleges Are Breaking Records." *New York Times*, January 17, 2008 *www.nytimes.com/2008/01/17/education/17admissions.html* (accessed December 31, 2009).

Aspy, Cheryl B., Sara K. Vesely, Roy F. Oman, Saron Rodine, Ladonna Marshall, and Ken McLeroy. "Parental Communication and Youth Sexual Behavior." *Journal of Adolescence,* 30 no. 3 (2007): 449–466.

Bandura, Albert. *Social Learning Theory.* Engelwood Cliffs, NJ: Prentice-Hall, 1977.

Barboza, Gia, Elise Schiamberg, Lawrence B. Oehmke, James Korzeniewski, Lori A. Post, and Cedrick G. Heraux. "Individual Characteristics and the Multiple Contexts of Adolescent Bullying: An Ecological Perspective." *Journal of Youth and Adolescence*, 38 (2009): 101–121.

Burns, James J., Mathew Sadof, and Depak Kamat. "Managing the Adolescent with a Chronic Illness." *Psychiatric Annals*, 36 no. 10 (2006): 715–719.

Butner, Jonathan, Cynthia A. Berg, and Peter Osborn, et al. "Parent-Adolescent Discrepancies in Adolescents' Competence and the Balance of Adolescent Autonomy and Adolescent and Parent Well-Being in the Context of Type 1 Diabetes." *Developmental Psychology*, 45 no. 3 (2009): 835–849.

Cox Communication in Partnership with the National Center for Missing & Exploited Children (NCMEC) and John Walsh. "Cox Communications Teen Internet Safety Survey, Wave II, Research Findings" *www.cox.com/takeCharge/includes/docs/survey_results_2007.ppt* (March 2007).

Dailey, Rene M., "Confirmation in Parent-Adolescent Relationships and Adolescent Openness: Toward Extending Confirmation Theory." *Communication Monographs*, 73 no. 4 (2006): 434–458.

Davis, Harry, and Frank A. Treiber, "Perceived Stress, Heart Rate, and Blood Pressure among Adolescents with Family Members Deployed in Operation Iraqi Freedom." *Military Medicine*, 172 no. 1 (2007): 40–44.

Drummet, Amy Reinkober, Marilyn Coleman, and Susan Cable. "Military Families under Stress: Implications for Family Life Education." *Family Relations*, 52.3 (2003): 279–290.

Ekman, Paul, Wallace V. Friesen, and Maureen O' Sullivan. "Smiles When Lying." *Journal of Personality and Social Psychology*, 54 no. 3 (1988): 414–420.

Elder, Glen H., Jr., Tri Van Nguyen, and Avshalom Caspi. "Linking Family Hardship to Children's Lives." *Child Development*, 56 (1985): 361–375.

Engels, Rutger, C.M.E, Catrin Finkenauer, and Dyana C. van Kooten. "Lying Behavior, Family Functioning and Adjustment in Early Adolescence." *Journal of Youth and Adolescence*, 35 (2006): 949–958.

Finkel, Lisa B., Michelle L. Kelley, and Jayne Ashby. "Geographic Mobility, Family, and Maternal Variables as Related to the Psychosocial Adjustment of Military Children." *Military Medicine*, 168.12 (2003): 1019–1024.

Flanagan, Constance A., and Jacquelynne S. Eccles. "Changes in Parents' Work Status and Adolescents' Adjustment at School." *Child Development*, 64 (1993): 246–257.

Frederick, Christina M., and Kristy A. Bradley. "A Different Kind of Normal? Psychological and Motivational Characteristics of Young Adult Tattooers and Body Piercers." *North American Journal of Psychology*, 2 no. 2 (2000): 380–391.

Galambos, Nancy L., and Rainer K. Silbereisen. "Income Change, Parental Life Outlook, and Adolescent Expectations for Job Success." *Journal of Marriage and the Family*, 49 (1987): 141–149.

Giarelli, Ellen, Barbara A. Bernhardt, Rita Mack, and Reed E. Pyeritz. "Adolescent's Transition to Self-Management of a Chronic Genetic Disorder." *Qualitative Health Research*, 18 no. 4 (2008): 441–457.

Glassbrenner, Donna, and Tony Jianqiang Ye. "Driver Cell Phone Use in 2006—Overall Results." Traffic Safety Facts, Washington, DC:NHTSA's National Center for Statistics and Analysis, July 2007, DOT HS 810 790.

Goldstein, Sara E., Pamela E. Davis-Kean, and Jaquelynne S. Eccles. "Parents, Peers, and Problem Behavior: A Longitudinal Investigation of the Impact of Relationship Perceptions and Characteristics on the Development of Adolescent Problem Behavior." *Developmental Psychology,* 41 no. 2 (2005): 401–413.

Guerrero, Laura K., and Walid A. Afifi. "Some Things Are Better Left Unsaid: Topic Avoidance in Family Relationships." *Communication Quarterly,* 43 (1995): 276–296.

Harris Interactive. A Cable in the Classroom & Common Sense Media Poll, "Parenting Moves Online: Parents' Internet Actions and Attitudes." (2007). *http://i.ciconline.org/poll/Parenting%20Online%20 Data1.pdf*

Hartos, Jessica L., Patricia Eitel, Denise L. Haynie, and Bruce G. Simons-Morton. "Can I Take the Car? Relations among Parenting Practices and Adolescent Problem-Driving Practices." *Journal of Adolescent Research,* 15, no. 3 (2000): 352–367.

Hawk, Skyler T., Loes Keijsers, William W. Hale, III, and Wim Meuss. "Mind Your Own Business! Longitudinal Relations Between Perceived Privacy Invasion and Adolescent-Parent Conflict." *Journal of Family Psychology,* 23.4 (2009): 511–520.

Heppner, Mary J., and P. Paul Heppner. "On Men and Work: Taking the Road Less Traveled." *Journal of Career Development*, 36 no. 1 (2009): 49–67.

Institute of Education Sciences (ies) National Center for Education Statistics (NCES). Digest of Education Statistics: 2008. *http://nces.ed.gov /programs/digest/d08/* (accessed December 13, 2009).

Institute of Education Sciences (ies) National Center for Education Statistics (NCES). Fast Facts. *http://nces.ed.gov/fastFacts/display .asp?id=98* (accessed December 13, 2009).

Insurance Institute for Highway Safety (IIHS). "Teenagers." Fatality Facts 2008, *www.iihs.org/research/fatality_facts_2008/teenagers.html* (accessed December 25, 2009).

Kahlbaugh, Patricia E., and Jeannette M. Haviland. "Nonverbal Communication Between Parents and Adolescents: A Study of Approach and Avoidance Behaviors." *Journal of Nonverbal Behavior*, 18 no. 1 (1994): 91–113.

Kail, Robert V., and John C. Cavanaugh. "Rites of Passage: Physical and Cognitive Development in Adolescence." Chap. 8 in *Human Development: A Life-Span View*, 5th ed. Belmont, CA: Wadsworh Cengage Learning, 2010.

Kerr, Margaret, and Hakan Stattin. "What Parents Know, How They Know It, and Several Forms of Adolescent Adjustment: Further Support for a Reinterpretation of Monitoring." *Developmental Psychology*, 36 no. 3 (2000): 366–380.

Ketchum Global Research Network, Prepared for Cox Communications and the National Center for Missing and Exploited Children and NetSmartz. "Parents' Internet Monitoring Study." (2005). *www.netsmartz.org/safety/statistics.htm*

Lempers, Jacques D., Dania Clark-Lempers, and Ronald L. Somons. "Economic Hardship, Parenting, and Distress in Adolescence." *Child Development*, 60 (1989): 25–39.

Madsen, Stephanie D. "Parents' Management of Adolescents' Romantic Relationships Through Dating Rules: Gender Variations and Correlates of Relationship Qualities." *Journal of Youth and Adolescence*, 37 (2008): 1044–1058.

Mazur, Michelle A., and Ebesu Hubbard. "'Is There Something I Should Know?': Topic Avoidant Responses in Parent-Adolescent Communication." *Communication Reports*, 17 no. 1 (2004): 27–37.

McCartt, Anne T., Eric R. Teoh, Michele Fields, Keli A. Braitman, and Laurie A. Hellinga. *Graduated Licensing Laws and Fatal Crashes of Teenage Drivers: A National Study*. Arlington, VA: Insurance Institute for Highway Safety, May 2009.

Miller, Kim S., Beth A. Kotchick, Shannon Dorsey, Rex Forehand, and Anissa Y. Ham. "Family Communication about Sex: What Are Parents Saying and Are Their Adolescents Listening?" *Family Planning Perspectives*, 30 no. 5 (1998): 218–235.

Miller, Patrick W. *Body Language: An Illustrated Introduction for Teachers*. Munster, IN: Miller, Patrick W. and Associates, 2005.

Mmari, Kristen, Kathleen M. Roche, May Sudhinaraset, and Robert Blum. "When a Parent Goes Off to War: Exploring the Issues Faced by Adolescents and Their Families." *Youth & Society*, 40 no. 4 (2009): 455–475.

Mosisa, Abraham, and Steven Hippie. U.S. Department of Labor, U.S. Bureau of Labor Statistics. "Trends in Labor Force Participation in the United States." *Monthly Labor Review*, 129 no. 10 (2006): 35–57.

Mounts, Nina S. "Parental Management of Adolescent Peer Relationship in Context: The Role of Parenting Style." *Journal of Family Psychology*, 16 no. 1 (2002): 58–69.

Mounts, Nina S., and Hyun-Soo Kim. "Expectations for Parental Management of Dating in an Ethnically Diverse Sample of Early Adolescents." *Journal of Adolescent Research*, 24 no. 5 (2009): 521–560.

National Association for College Admission Counseling (NACAC). "College Admission Trends Relatively Steady Though Increased Applications and Economy Produce Slight Changes." 2009. *www.nacanet.org/AboutNACAC/PressRoom/2009/Pages/09soca.aspx* (accessed December 13, 2009).

National Highway Traffic Safety Administration (NHTSA). "Young Drivers." Traffic Safety Facts 2008 Data. Washington, DC: NHTSA's National Center for Statistics and Analysis, 2008. DOT HS 811 169.

National Highway Traffic Safety Administration (NHTSA). "NHTSA Policy and FAQs on Cellular Phone Use While Driving." October 2, 2009. *www.nhtsa.dot.gov/portal/site/nhtsa/template,MAXIMIZE/menuitem.5475ba83ef* (accessed December 24, 2009).

Netlingo. "The List of Chat Acronyms & Text Message Shorthand." *www.netlingo.com/emailsh.cfm* (accessed July 8, 2008).

Noller, Patricia, and Stephen Bagi. "Parent-Adolescent Communication." *Journal of Adolescence*, 8.2 (1985): 125–144.

Ortiz, Larry Paul Andres, and Michael P. Farrell. "Father's Unemployment and Adolescent's Self-Concept." *Adolescence*, 28 no. 112 (1993): 937–949.

Pai, Ahna L. H., Rachel Neff Greenley, Amy Lewandowski, Dennis Drotar, Eric Youngstrom, and Catherine Cant Peterson. "A Meta-Analytic Review of the Influence of Pediatric Cancer on Parent and Family Functioning." *Journal of Family Psychology*, 21 no. 3 (2007): 407–415.

Pease, Alan, and Barbara Pease. *The Definitive Book of Body Language.* New York: Bantam Dell, 2006.

Preti, Antonio, Claudia Pinna, Silvia Nocco, Emanuela Melliri, Simona Pilia, Donatella R. Petretto, and Carmelo Masala. "Body of Evidence: Tattoos, Body Piercing, and Eating Disorder Symptoms among Adolescents." *Journal of Psychoanalytic Research*, 61 no. 4 (2006): 561–566.

Sarkar, Shelia, and Marie Andreas. "Acceptance of and Engagement in Risky Driving Behaviors by Teenagers." *Adolescence*, 39 no. 156 (2004): 687–700.

Schilling, Lynne S., Margaret Grey, and Kathleen A. Knafl. "The Concept of Self-Management of Type 1 Diabetes in Children and Adolescents: An Evolutionary Concept Analysis." *Journal of Advanced Nursing*, 37 no. 1 (2002): 87–89.

Silverberg Koerner, Susan, Sara Wallace, Stephanie Jacobs Lehman, and Meghan Raymond. "Mother-to-Daughter Disclosure after Divorce: Are There Costs and Benefits?" *Journal of Child and Family Studies*, 11 no. 4 (2002): 469–483.

Site Admin. "Understanding Text Messaging Abbreviations." *www.funnelideas.com*, 2008. *http://funnelideas.com/solution.asp? 40-Understanding-text-message-abbreviations* (accessed July 8, 2008).

Soens, Bart, Maarten Vansteenkiste, Willy Lens, Koen Luyckx, Luc Gossens, Wim Beyers, and Richard M. Ryan. "Conceptualizing Parental Autonomy Support: Adolescent Perceptions of Promotion of Independence Versus Promotion of Volitional Functioning." *Developmental Psychology*, 43 no. 3 (2007): 633–646.

Subrahmanyam, Kaveri, and Patricia Greenfeld. "Online Communication and Adolescent Relationships." *The Future of Children*, 18 no. 1 (2008): 119–146.

Valkenburg, Patti M., and Jochen Peter. "Preadolescents' and Adolescents Online Communication and Their Closeness to Friends." *Developmental Psychology*, 43 no. 2 (2007): 267–277.

Van Beek, Yolanda, and Judith Semon Dubas, "Age and Gender Differences in Decoding Basic and Non-Basic Facial Expressions in Late Childhood and Early Adolescence." *Journal of Nonverbal Behavior*, 32 (2008): 37–82.

Wadsworth, Martha E., and Bruce E. Compas. "Coping with Family Conflict and Economic Strain: The Adolescent Perspective." *Journal of Research on Adolescence*, 12 no. 2 (2002): 243–274.

Webopedia. 2008. "Text Messaging Abbreviations: A Guide to Understanding Online Chat Acronyms & Smiley Faces." *www.webopedia.com /quick_ref/textmessageabbreviations.asp* (accessed July 8, 2008).

Yu, Shuli, Rebecca Clemens, Hongmei Yang, Xiaoming Li, Bonita Stanton, Lynette Deveaux, Sonja Lunn, Lesley Cottrell, and Carole Harris. "Youth and Parental Perceptions of Parental Monitoring and Parent-Adolescent Communication, Youth Depression, and Youth Risk Behaviors." *Social Behavior and Personality*, 34 no. 10 (2006): 1297–1310.

Zimmerman, Toni Schindler, Leslie Parker Northern, Stephanie Crandall Seng, and John W. Grogan. "Marital Equality When Fathers Stay Home." *Initiatives*, 59 no. 1 (1999): 45–63.

INDEX

About the Authors

Barbara R. Greenberg, PhD, is a clinical psychologist who specializes in the treatment of teens and their families. She was the program director of an adolescent inpatient unit at a private northeastern psychiatric hospital for twenty-one years before dedicating herself to private outpatient practice. Barbara is a respected writer, speaker, and consultant on teen issues. She resides in the northeast. This book serves as a culmination of her years of research and direct work with hundreds of adolescents. She is proud to say, she really understands what they are saying!

Jennifer A. Powell-Lunder, PsyD is a clinical psychologist who specializes in the treatment of teens and their families. She is currently the program director of an adolescent inpatient unit at a private northeastern psychiatric hospital. She is also an adjunct Professor of Psychology at Pace University and maintains a private outpatient practice. Jennifer is a respected writer, speaker, and consultant on teen issues. She resides with her family including their black Labrador retriever in the northeast. Jennifer is inspired daily by the teens with whom she works. She appreciates their acknowledgment that she really does get it.

When You Don't Have Time for Anything Else

Visit our Cereal for Supper blog and join other over-inundated, under-celebrated, multi-tasking moms for an (almost) daily allowance of parenting advice—and absolution.

You won't learn how to make handmade Martha Stewart–inspired hankie holders or elaborate gourmet dinners—but you will find heaping spoonfuls of support and a few laughs along the way!

Sign up for our newsletter now at
www.adamsmedia.com/blog/parenting
And get our FREE Top Ten Recipes for Picky Eaters!